BEST PRACTICE

Programme Management
based on MSP

AN INTRODUCTION

VHP

VAN HAREN PUBLISHING

Programme Management

Based on MSP

AN INTRODUCTION

Bert Hedeman
Gabor Vis van Heemst

Van Haren
PUBLISHING

Colophon

Title:	Programme Management based on MSP - an introduction
Authors:	Bert Hedeman (Insights International b.v.)
	Gabor Vis van Heemst (Getronics PinkRoccade)
Quality Audit Team	Ad van den Akker (Lagant)
	Hans Fredriksz (ISES International)
	Wil Hendrickx (Lagant)
	Sander van der Meijs (KPMG Information RiskManagement)

From MSP-User-group Netherland:
René de Bie (Getronics PinkRoccade)
Robert Knoop (ABNAmro)
Hans van Leeuwen(Getronics PinkRoccade)
Wim van der Weijden (ETD ExperienceTheDifference)
Wilbert Wijns (NedTrain)

From Interest Group Programme management, PMI:
Hans Camstra (Big River Innovation)
Rix Hof (Getronics PinkRoccade)
Jan Hoogenraad (Nederlandse Spoorwegen)
Theo van der Tak (Twynstra Gudde)

UK Edition:
Andy Taylor (Aquila Business Services Ltd) Chief Examiner MSP
Alan Ferguson (AFA)
Elaine Taylor (Society of Indexers)

Publisher:	Van Haren Publishing, Zaltbommel, www.vanharen.net
ISBN:	90 77212 06 X
Copyright:	© 2006 Van Haren Publishing, Zaltbommel, The Netherlands
Version:	First edition, first impression, February 2006
Design & layout:	DTPresto grafisch ontwerp & layout, Zeewolde - NL

For more information on Van Haren Publishing, e-mail: info@vanharen.net

Foreword

In recent years, project work has become a well known concept. Things don't just happen by themselves, but rather by applying the special skills that are being developed. As people learn how to carry out their roles more efficiently and get more experience with projects, it's clear that Project Managers can no longer be ignored in this fast-changing world.

Why programmes? What is the difference between a programme and a project? Why create such an enormous structure, let's get someone else to do it! Is it just so we can justify a higher salary? These comments are often heard from people who are involved in implementing programme management or dealing with projects for the first time. However, we have had positive and promising experiences with programmes and programme management. In 1995, I experienced at first hand the shortcomings of a project when making changes to an organization as a whole, being suddenly dependent on many factors that couldn't be managed as projects. I welcomed the MSP tool when it became available in 1999 and still use it with great pleasure and good results.

Increasingly organizations incorporate their important goals and requirements into their project calendars every year. By organizing projects into project portfolios, the use of staff and resources is optimized. This is not the case where the connection between projects and the organizational changes necessary to achieve goals have to be managed; the subsequent results are poorer. We will really only achieve programme levels if we also incorporate the management of benefits that are required to achieve the strategic goal. This is still a challenge for many organizations.

Looking back over the past few years, it is clear that programme management cannot be ignored in organizing and managing strategic changes. It is a natural development in project management where the occurrence, connection and coordination of projects, changes and output are managed integrally in an organization. No doubt many organizations already have the services of a Chief Projects Officer (CPO) at the highest level, who is responsible for the success of strategic projects and the outcome of corporate projects.

'Programme Management: An Introduction based on MSP' provides a very useful book on programme management and the use of MSP as a method of implementing projects. The combination of MSP as a tool, and programme management as a method of achieving strategic change, makes the book relevant for a wide audience. Both those who define the strategic goals of organizations, and those playing a role in their realization, would do well to read it.

The authors describe various aspects of programme management: They deal with all management roles, the management processes, and the management of projects, changes and output in relation to strategy. The title describes different approaches that may used and the material benefits from descriptions of relevant instruments.

Perhaps even more than with other programme methods, whilst MSP is a comprehensive technique, it is the skill of the Programme Manager and his staff that determines success. Method alone is not enough; as they say in England: "A fool with a tool still remains a fool". In this book we have tried to show you not only the method but also something of the skills required for successful programme management. If you finish the book having learned nothing new then we congratulate you for expertise of two vital elements needed for successful programme management

MSP is the current 'de facto standard' for programme management in the Netherlands. I congratulate the authors Bert Hedeman and Gabor Vis van Heemst on this book, their second standard work following their book 'Project Management, An introduction based on PRINCE2™'.

Gerrit C.L. Koch CPD,
Berenschot

Contents

As a guide

The book 'Programme Management, An introduction based on MSP' is intended as a handbook for practical use when working in and with programmes. It describes a process-type approach for managing programmes, together with a number of aspects or 'principles' required for this.

The description of the process-type approach is based on the programme management method MSP (Managing Successful Programmes). MSP was developed in 1999 by the Central Computer and Telecommunication Agency (CCTA). The CCTA, since renamed the Office of Government Commerce (OGC), is an agency of the British Government. The MSP method gives a pragmatic approach to managing programmes. It helps organizations to realize corporate strategies and goals in their organizations, as well as achieving innovation, implementing new management and ensuring planned added value. The principles for managing programmes have been developed over several years and applied within several fields. These principles can be applied to all sorts of programmes, from developing complex housing problems to corporate reorganizations and e-commerce services.

The methodology has been developed in consultation with public and private companies and fits in with the contemporary corporate environment. It takes account of fast changes that can take place both in and outside the organizations. The method is also easy to apply in those cases where businesses wish to cooperate in order to achieve joint objectives.

OGC has also developed the ITIL and PRINCE2 methodologies in the past. PRINCE2 is a generic project management methodology for all types of project. MSP and PRINCE2 are process-oriented methodologies, thus fitting in entirely with one another. OGC brought out a new version of the MSP manual in 2003.

The contents of this book easily satisfy the theoretical demands required to pass the MSP Foundation examination. Additional practical experience is required for the MSP Intermediate and Practitioner examinations.

This book has been written for Programme Directors, Programme Managers, Business Change Managers and Sponsoring Group members, and anyone else involved in setting-up or implementing a programme. The book provides a framework for setting-up, structuring and implementing programmes and is certainly not intended to cover all areas of programme management; several other good books have already been written on these subjects.

For the sake of clarity, this book follows the introduction as used in the OGC manual 'Managing Successful Programmes' and the terminology is also based on that of MSP. In addition to the MSP method, consideration has also been given to managing and realizing changes.
An example is also given in the form of a case study showing the organization of the most important management products, and help given in risk identification and performance measurement methods.

Finally, we wish to point out that wherever the book makes reference to people as 'he' or 'his' , this can of course be taken to mean "she" or "her".

We would like to thank all the reviewers who have contributed to the quality of this book.

Bert Hedeman, Gabor Vis van Heemst

1 Introduction

1.1 Implementing change

Change is part of everyday life. People change their place of residence or work, children leave home or the garden is changed; it's part of life. The increasing social environment appears to bring us more choices, and these lead to more changes, which follow one another in ever-faster succession. This is also the case in organizations. Globalization, increased competition and changes in clients' demands are just a few examples businesses are faced with. As the saying goes 'change is the only constant'.

But the implementation of change is not easy. Change always involves risks and disadvantages, as well as advantages. They are dependent on many other factors; as soon as you change one item, you have to change the other factors too. Various parties are also involved, with different interests and priorities. Many changes are unsuccessful, cause much more trouble or are seen with hindsight to be more painful than necessary. There is, therefore, a clear need for a method of implementing change and thus increasing the chance of success. Programme management is such a method for successful and structured change implementation.

1.2 The programme management structure

The implementation of change in organizations requires a focused vision towards that change and a structured approach, coordination and management of the change activities. Programme management delivers this approach and helps to reach such a vision through a defined organization structure, phasing, processes, activities, products and the method of thinking. The methodology puts the organization and staff in a position to implement changes and to deal in a controlled way with uncertainties and upheavals that will appear during the process. The structure is also a base for development and completion of the necessary skills in order to implement the changes.

Programmes are different from projects. Whereas projects deliver products or services, programme management is based on implementing changes or realizing added value for the organization. Programme management is thus not only based on coordinating projects necessary for the changes, but also on implementing and securing the changes in the organization and realizing the benefits envisaged by the organization.

1.3 When should programme management be used?

With many projects and activities in an organization, the relationships between these and their dependencies on the (often complex) environment mean that change management demands a great deal of effort from the line organization and operational management.

Carrying out changes with a limited capacity to realize them all has led to a need to find another method of control for managing changes. The characteristics of this approach are that we are dealing with phases characterised with much uncertainty and risk, and also with a clear link to the strategy of the business. Programme management can make a particular contribution in situations whereby:

- There is a lack of clarity as to the goals to be achieved
- Complex changes need to be implemented
- There are strong dependencies between many projects and activities
- The available capacity is limited
- A turbulent environment exists within which the changes that are to be implemented
- There are many risks connected with implementing the changes
- There are various possibilities for implementing the changes
- The outcome of various projects is needed to make changes possible
- Management has to spend too much time on implementing the changes
- Implementing the changes has too great an impact on the primary processes, jeopardizing continuity
- This requires co-ordination of several initiatives, with common ground with existing business processes.

In summary, programme management can be used in situations where relations between the specialities of groups of projects are complex and where efficient use must be made of the shared capacity. Programme management can also make a positive contribution where the total costs of the change must be limited and managed, and where the focus on the objectives and benefits must be realized without too much disturbance to the primary process. Another reason for switching to programme management can be that senior management has to spend less time on changes.

1.4　Advantages of programme management

The benefits of programme management come from co-ordinated change management, governing the mutual dependencies between projects and activities, and a central focus on realizing the benefits. The most important advantages are:

- Effective realization of changes by an integral (planned and managed) approach to various elements of change, without existing business processes being disturbed unnecessarily
- Effective response to strategic initiatives by bridging the 'gap' between strategy and the realization of projects and activities
- Focus on the goals of changes by providing a framework for senior managers in the organization whereby they can govern and manage the change process
- Efficient resource management whereby programme management provides mechanisms for project priorities and project integration
- Better risk management by placing the complexity and range of the Project Portfolio in a wider context
- Realization of objectives and benefits by setting-up a formal process of Benefit Management. Important steps in the process are: identifying, defining, monitoring and measuring the benefits.
- Effective management of business objectives (Business Case). Setting-up and maintaining the Business Case allows constant appraisal of the best solutions from a business point of view and whether the continued implementation of changes is still desired

Gradual transition from current to new business processes. The transition from the current organization to the new way of working is a separate aspect of programme management.

1.5 Definitions

It is important to establish a clear framework of definitions for each methodology. Table 1.1 shows the most important ones used within programme management.

Definition	Description
Benefit	The quantifiable and measurable improvement resulting from an outcome which is perceived as positive by a stakeholder and which will normally have a tangible value expressed in monetary or resource terms. Benefits are expected when a change is conceived. Benefits are realised as a result of activities undertaken to effect the change.
Blueprint	A description of the future environment that management wishes to achieve in implementing the programme to deliver the capability described in the Vision Statement. This contains, amongst other things, a description of the people and their skills, working practices and processes, organizational structures, quality systems, information and reporting systems, and the necessary technical infrastructure.
Capability	A service, function or process which the organization can exploit to realize benefits
Change	The alteration of a situation from the current to a new state.
Enabler	Project or activity with the goal of delivering an envisaged outcome but that which of itself may not deliver any specific benefit.
End goal	Unique strategic goal to be achieved with the programme
Key Performance Indicator (KPI)	An important characteristic of an operation, service or function in a particular environment, based on which performance is measured. It is the standard against which something is measured or a goal realized.
Mission	The legitimacy of the organisation's existence
Outcome	A product or service brought about by an enabler. The effect of a change the measurement of which is a benefit
Performance	A condition of a quality of an object in a specified environment.
Status quo	The total of the organization's current capabilities without any changes incorporated
Transition	Implementation and embedding the new or changed capabilities into the business organization so that they become business as usual and realize the expected benefits.
Vision	A description prepared from the business's perspective as to what the programme must deliver.

Table 1.1 Summary of the most important definitions in programme management

A complete summary of the definitions used is given in the list of definitions at the back of the book. Figure 1.1 shows the relations between the various definitions.

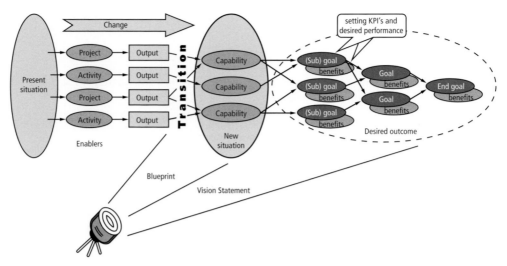

Fig 1.1 Relationship between various terms

1.6   About this book

This book deals mainly with:

- Various characteristics and concepts of programme management
- The roles and associated tasks, responsibilities and authorities of the various parties implementing changes, and the skills required for these roles
- The most important processes, activities and products as part of the programme management approach
- The manner in which the changes can be carried out.

This approach is intended as a framework for implementing changes. Situations differ for each case and organization to such an extent that a rigidly prescribed methodology is inappropriate. The methodology must always be applied according to the situation and combined with plenty of common sense and a good feel for the environment.

The MSP methodology described in this book must not be seen as a methodology taking the place of others, but rather complementing other methodologies. MSP lays down the structure within which other methods and approaches can find their place. See chapter 18 in which various approaches for change are described.

The introductory chapters 2 and 3 deal with change management and the differences between projects and programmes. The book is then divided into two parts which are

1. Principles of Programme management:
- Organization and leadership
- Benefits management
- Stakeholder management and communication
- Risk management and issue resolution
- Programme planning and control

- Business Case management
- Quality management

2. Programme Management Processes:
- Identifying a programme
- Defining a programme
- Governing a programme
- Managing the portfolio
- Managing benefits
- Closing a programme

The book also contains some annexes:
- Realizing changes
- Roles of the Programme Management Team
- Performance measuring methods
- List of definitions
- Organization of management products
- Translation list
- Literature list
- Reference list
- Contact addresses

2 Managing phases of the change

2.1 Strategic changes

This chapter of the book deals with strategic changes. But what is a strategic change? It is a change within an organization, which determines the development and/or continued existence of the organization itself. This involves how a company is oriented. Examples of strategic changes are:

- Creating a new organization following a merger or takeover
- Procuring and implementing facilities or services
- Reacting to changing situations that are a challenge or a threat to operational management
- Considerably increasing client service levels whereby primary processes and work procedures also need adjusting
- Complying with revised regulations or laws.

> "When you lend an ear but no more hear, no sighing, no breathing and no heart beating, you may assume that something is dead. But as long as it is still flapping and moving, it's still alive. This is so with all organisms, people, animals, plants and also organizations. Change is inherent to life. Living organizations are always moving."
>
> Wim Dik, previously Senior Executive at KPN,
> "Kwaliteit in Bedrijf", September 2000

Small changes in maintenance or enhancements to existing work processes are not generally implemented via separate change phases. This type of change is normally dealt with and implemented parallel to and during the primary working process - "business as usual".

2.2 Reasons for strategic changes

There are many different types of programme but what they all have in common is that they involve change. This change can be to the business processes and/or the environment, and can become necessary for reasons such as changes in the political climate, legislation or technological developments (e.g. the Internet). Modifying objectives from the business itself might also make programmes and programme management desirable. Examples of this are the need for globalization, quality demands and industry standards and improvement in product quality or services (see figure 2.1).

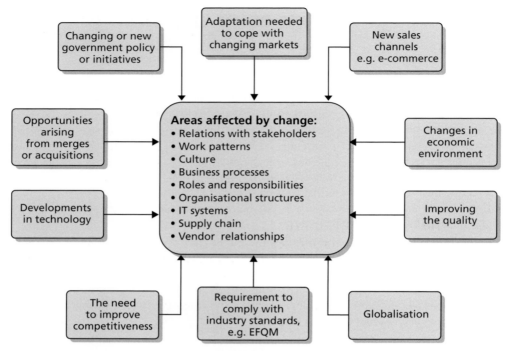

Fig. 2.1 Reasons for starting a programme (© Crown copyright 2003 reproduced under licence from HMSO)

2.3 Initiating the phase of a change

Each kind of change requires its own approach. It is unwise to implement changes gradually in a situation where a lot of money is lost every day; something has to be done straightaway. On the other hand, there are changes - certainly in situations that can be planned - where it is right to proceed carefully and implement changes with caution. It is therefore important to recognize urgency as well as focus on the environment to find a suitable approach.

To achieve the objectives of these changes, it is necessary to find a way of managing the change phase, particularly when we consider the often complex environment of programmes and projects.

Whatever the reason, at a certain point, senior management within an organization will develop a new vision from which strategic and tactical choices will be made, and which will guide the priorities set by the business for current or future investments and changes. The renewed choices will lead to one or more programmes, whereby each programme vision is linked to the business vision and the programme goal linked to the goals of the business.

It is of vital importance when initiating the change phases to check thoroughly that the organization is ready for the change and has the resources to change.

Changes have an impact on all those concerned, both inside and outside the organization. The risk of changes made in quick succession in an organization is that people will grow tired of change. In order to get a good picture of whether an organizational change has a chance of success, senior management must, among other things, pay attention to the extent to which a business can be changed. They must plan changes prior to them being implemented, set the goals and objectives for the changes, and identify any showstoppers.

There must be a continuous and joint understanding of the necessity for the change and the new situation one is trying to achieve. Management must realize that a considerable enabler is needed to implement changes and that all stakeholders should understand the consequences of the changes for the organization and for their own working environment. Management need to keep in mind the dependence between the change to be implemented and other initiatives. They must ensure that normal business management is continued while the change is being implemented: "We are still open for business while structural alterations are being carried out".

2.4   What is a programme?

The term 'programme' is used in many ways and can be confusing. It is therefore important to use unambiguous and clear definitions for the terms 'programme' and 'programme management'. This book defines the word 'programme' as:

'the temporary organization of a series of connected projects and activities for realizing one or more strategically important pre-defined objectives'

and defines 'programme management' as:

'the co-ordinated organization, management and implementation of a series of connected projects and activities for realizing one or more strategically important pre-defined objectives'.

An important difference when compared with a project is the focus on realizing objectives. There are specific processes and principles within programme management that concentrate on these objectives.

2.5   Types of programmes

Each programme is unique in what it aims to deliver and the circumstances under which this is carried out. Figure 2.2 shows examples of types of programmes and areas where changes are carried out.

2.5.1 Construction, engineering and ICT

It is characteristic of this environment to be unambiguous and the results to be delivered are often clearly described and specified. It is clear what must take place and often how much time and energy will be required. There will be few major changes while the project is being carried out. This will involve the preparation and completion of products, with the focus more on result-oriented work rather than just the objectives of the project.

This type of programme differs from projects in the distribution of tasks, authority and responsibilities. With a project, the manager (the Project Manager) is responsible for producing project results that are within the budget, produced on time and can be used by the client to realize the Business Case. With a programme, the manager (Programme Manager) is responsible for the above, as well as for delivering the results and (partial) realization of the Business Case.

This may, for example, deal with the implementation and development of a new computing centre, or the introduction of a new product where development will be reviewed after a few months to see if it can be included in the standard range.

2.5.2 Change management

This concerns programmes for carrying out changes in an organization from a strategic viewpoint, with effectiveness and efficiency as starting points for the change. Consideration is therefore given to the realization of benefits. This type of change is often less clear than the previous type of programme, but there is still a reasonably good vision of what must be done. The chances for change are greater, but the changes will generally be across the board and dealt with reactively. More components will become clear throughout the implementation period and these can be managed as projects.

Examples of this type of programme may include changing a department to accommodate the demands of a new market, or the reorganization phase following a merger or takeover.

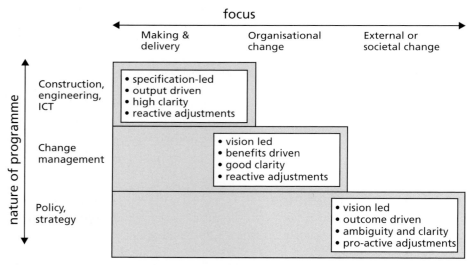

Fig. 2.2 Types of change (© Crown copyright 2003 reproduced under licence from HMSO)

2.5.3 Policy and strategy

A strategic programme consists of a set of projects and individual activities for realizing an organization's strategic objectives. This is also based on a vision, but deals much more with reaching the higher strategic goals than just the benefits.

The environment is ambivalent, so there is no clear picture of what must be done. Negotiations are often carried out in this case to find clarity for the procedure that follows. The frameworks are more flexible and the entire scope of the changes is dealt with carefully. While this is being done, parts of the tasks will become clearer and they can also be managed as a change phase.

What is remarkable is that the objectives from the various projects might conflict with one another, but they will still support the co-ordinating goals in the wider context. The challenge here is to have the various objectives balanced in such a way that the strategic objectives can be achieved.

An example of a strategic programme is setting-up an e-business. Implementation is often only driven by a vision of the final outcome. A lot of uncertainties exist in the beginning and the Programme Manager will react pro-actively to possible future developments. The programme could involve the setting-up of systems, motivating clients to work with e-business, preparing the organization for e-business and setting-up a helpdesk.

2.5.4 Multi-organization programmes

This type of programme is characterized by the co-operation of various organizations in managing or sponsoring the programme. These organizations might have the same or different backgrounds (industry or market). The reason for the co-operation is the joint goals and benefits, which the organization cannot achieve on its own.

Such programmes are common in the logistics sector, where the concept 'providing the complete package' is becoming more and more important. Far-reaching co-operation is required here in supply chain management, to serve the final consumer efficiently. In these programmes, each partner supplies the input for realizing the joint vision. Each participating organization maintains its own business goals that are to be achieved, as well as the joint vision of the partnership.

Other well-known examples include the private-public ventures where local government and private businesses work together to develop areas that would be much more difficult to launch without direct co-operation.

2.6   Programmes in their context

Programmes are not independent; everything is connected. A programme is part of the business organization where the change needs to take place, and its goals are a derivative of those of the business. The business goals are determined by internal and external factors such as political, market and corporate technological developments. From the programme, the projects and activities are initiated and carried out from a coherent vision of the end result. These projects and activities will deliver results, which together will provide the capabilities necessary to implement the changes in business processes. In the end, the business organization must achieve the intended benefits with the changes implemented (see figure 2.3). It is therefore important for a Programme Management Team to get a good picture of the environment in which the programme is to be implemented.

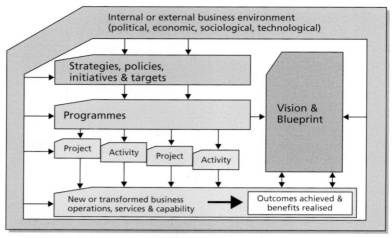

Fig. 2.3 Programmes in their context (© Crown copyright 1999 reproduced under licence from HMSO)

2.7   Changes and programme management

Although there is no standard concept for a successful change, a structured work method will increase the chances of success and reduce the risks. Many organizations opt to have their change phases realized not via the business organization itself, but by using a programme.

A programme management methodology delivers a set of management processes and principles with which a Programme Management Team can complete a change successfully. It offers the possibility of dividing the programme into manageable chunks, making the change easier to handle and offering more opportunity to ensure the client remains involved. Programme management allows the investment in normal business operations' time to be limited to what is really needed, so the business organization is disturbed as little as possible. The choice to implement a change via a separate programme instead of through the business organization itself is determined by the cost-benefit ratio. The advantages (or the reduction of disadvantages) of setting-up and managing a programme must measure up against the costs of that programme.

The programme will deliver, via the underlying projects, a number of results enabling the programme management team to implement the change (from 'current' to 'target'). The benefits can be realized from the changed situation, as defined at the beginning of the programme.

2.8   Critical success factors

There must be a good reason for carrying out the changes. An accepted image of the solution needs to be put in place by the most important people in the organization and this must be seen to be done. The Programme Manager should be involved and want the change without this being forced on him. He must be seen to work quickly and this should be a fixed feature of daily operations. Only then can changes actually be implemented and show their added value for the organization in the long term.

The following steps are conditions for successful implementation:

Make the necessity clear

Changes cost energy. This energy can only be released if there is a clear need for the change. This can be a possible threat or an opportunity, so it is also important to state and share this need for urgency.

Involving senior management

The choice of implementing changes depends largely on the image and experiences of the most important players within the organization. It is not sufficient for the need for change to be felt lower down in the organization or in middle management. The change is not viable if senior management cannot be convinced of the need for it; they must be behind the change and regard it as their problem.

Looking for an owner within senior management

Someone has to take responsibility for the change at senior management level. If everyone is the owner, then no-one is the owner, and nothing or very little will get done. It must be possible to address the owner at the appropriate management level; he's the figurehead, the 'champion', owner or standard-bearer of the change. There are several names, but they all mean the same, important thing: that this 'Senior Responsible Owner' bears managerial responsibility for the programme and is the real owner of the change. The change will have the best chance of success if the owner is also the *primus inter pares* (first amongst equals) from within the leading coalition of senior managers.

Clear and consistent vision of the final outcome

It is important that everyone involved in the change has the same image of the future and of why the change must take place. By sharing the vision and the Blueprint of the change, the parties involved can identify themselves more with the programme and what is happening. This is also the case with procuring and maintaining the use of staff and resources.

Clear tasks, responsibilities and authorities

One of the most numbing factors with project and programme management is that those involved do not know who is responsible for what, or who can be approached about what. Normally, nothing will happen if several people seem responsible, so establishing clear roles is a must.

Focus on added value

Realizing the benefits is a programme's primary objective. Managing the benefits, from identification through to receiving and measuring the added value, may cost a lot of time, money and management effort, but it is essential for implementing the change. Without this focus on the benefits, the change will have no drive and will soon get bogged down in haggling about what should happen.

Focus on the justification and the risks

There must be practical justification in order to implement a programme and there is no change without uncertainty. The justification and the risks must be established at the beginning of the programme and be tested and managed regularly during the programme.

Empowerment

Empowerment is an important condition for success. Empowerment means that those involved in the programme can make decisions and have sufficient powers and authority within the framework of the programme. This does not mean that each person might decide his own direction, but that all those involved may give as much of their own personal interpretation as possible within the business limitations necessary for realizing the objectives.

Planning, governing and monitoring the process

A structured change is not possible without process management. Changes must also be planned and require governing and monitoring.

Generating and celebrating quick wins

It's great to see that on paper the new way of working should improve the situation, but nothing is more convincing than these improvements actually happening. Celebrate the success and reward the successful. Do not leave this to chance, but consciously seek short-term successes; these are energy for the motor of change.

Communicating

Nothing is more frustrating than those involved not knowing what is going to happen. What does the change mean for the organization, how far ahead is the change, has the change already had an effect, and what does the change mean for me? It is not enough for the message to be spread but it is important that management acts in accordance with its own message, as a good example is worth following. Furthermore, it is essential to repeat the message again and again.

Securing the new work method

Changes that are not secured in the organization tend, after a time, to return to their original state. It can take years before new work methods become 'business as usual'. It is therefore essential to embed the changes into the organization's procedures and control systems.

2.9   Basic principles of MSP

MSP endorses all the aforementioned success factors for implementing changes. Specific issues of MSP in relation to other methodologies are:

- A description of the vision and a Blueprint of the new organization must be defined before starting to implement a programme and these are the main elements in planning and realizing the programme
- Identifying and establishing the added value for the organization, and ensuring they are measurable and then managing the added value so that this can be realized
- A focus on the justification and the risk: this is essential within the MSP philosophy and is the leading principle for programmes.

MSP also has a defined organizational structure with clearly described roles, each with their own set of tasks, responsibilities and authority. In the organization model, the Management Team is offered a structure to help guarantee as far as possible the involvement of senior management and stakeholders.

3 Programmes versus projects

Projects, large projects and programmes are all terms that cause much confusion. In practice, there appears to be a great lack of clarity as to the difference between the terms, partly because there has been great inflation in the past as to the function and role descriptions of people working in projects. Those who were Project Managers are now either: Programme Managers, Project Directors or Programme Directors.

Among the questions that must be clarified before we continue with programme management are: what is a project, what is a programme and what is the difference? What does programme management entail? What is the difference between a large project and a programme? What is multi-project management?

3.1 Project management

There are many different definitions of a project. According to Gert Wijnen and Geert Groote[1], a project is "a temporary result-oriented co-operation between persons where use is made of scarce resources". Teun van Aken[2] defines a project as "a series of connected activities carried out for the purpose of a pre-agreed outcome with a starting and finishing date, using limited resources and manpower, and usually of a unique nature". PRINCE2[3] defines a project as "a temporary organization set-up with the goal of delivering one or more business products according to a specified Business Case". A project according to the Nederlandse Competence Baseline (NCB)[4] is "a series of connected activities within a temporary organization for delivering a pre-defined outcome under set conditions".

These definitions differ regarding description but to a large extent are intrinsically related to one another. This book will use the NCB definition of what constitutes a project:

"a series of connected activities within a temporary organization for delivering a pre-defined outcome under set conditions".

Project management can be defined as:

"a co-ordinated organization and management of a series of connected activities for delivering a pre-defined outcome".

The characteristics of a project are:
- *Connected activities:* the connection between the activities comes from the goal of delivering the outcome as effectively as possible within set parameters.
- *Temporary organization:* the organization is set-up for the duration of the project.
- *Set conditions:* within pre-set parameters. With other definitions, this is restricted to limited or scarce resources. PRINCE2 links the conditions to practical justification.

- *Pre-defined:* a project involves a planned method of work stating in advance what must be delivered. The level of definition can vary. This will further transpire as necessary during the project.
- *Outcome:* this is the product or service delivered and transferred to the client organization.

3.2 Programme management

There are also several different definitions of the term 'programme'. According to Gert Wijnen, a programme is "a collection of temporary, connected and dynamic goals and enablers (including projects) and resources requiring management, as resources are limited and goals worthwhile". According to MSP, a programme is "a portfolio of projects and activities co-ordinated and managed as a unit in such a way that they achieve out-comes and realize benefits". The NCB definition of a programme is "a temporary series of connected projects and activities aimed at achieving a strategic goal".

Each of these definitions points to essential aspects of a programme. As described earlier, this book will use the following definition of a programme:

"a series of connected projects and activities within a temporary organization for delivering one or more strategically important pre-defined objectives".

Programme management can be defined as:

"the co-ordinated organization, management and implementation of a series of connected projects and activities for realizing one or more strategically important pre-defined objectives".

The most important characteristics of a programme are:
- *Connected projects and activities:* a programme involves more than just projects. As well as activities in projects, normal line management activities also need to be carried out in order to achieve the objectives.
- *Temporary organization:* the organization is set-up for the duration of the programme. This does not differ from a project in this respect, but the structure, tasks, responsibilities and authorities of those involved in a programme are more and different from those within a project.
- *Pre-defined:* this is also the same as for a project. The programme will not be seen to exist until the objectives that are to be achieved have been clearly defined. The defining parameters can be more or less detailed and will transpire further during the programme.
- *Objectives:* a programme will realize one or more objectives. With this, the programme is a substitute for the client's business organization. This means the programme runs longer than the related projects.
- *Strategic:* The term 'strategic objectives' implies that a large part of the organization is involved both in implementation and importance. It is due to this involvement, and the complexity involved, that the decision might be taken to implement a programme instead of having the strategic objectives carried out exclusively within the normal business operations.

An organization will set objectives that have to be realized by the programme. Therefore, as well as implementing a number of projects, the programme will have to develop a number of activities to make use of the results delivered by the projects. It will also have to implement the necessary changes in the business organization, which must be prepared to implement the changes. The results of the projects should be implemented in the normal business operations, with the new facilities successfully introduced as 'business as usual'. This new method must also be capable of delivering the objectives envisaged.

3.3   Various projects and programmes

Differences between a project and a programme are (see table 3.1):

- In contrast to a project whereby pre-defined results are delivered, a programme is intended to realize the objectives. A programme uses products and services from projects and activities in order to realize the objectives
- A programme differs from a project in its organizational structure, tasks, responsibilities and authorities. This different structure comes from the responsibility of a programme to realize the objectives
- A project has clear starting and finishing dates and ends on completion of the project delivery. A programme realizes objectives, meaning that the finishing date is less clear
- A programme runs a lot longer than a project. The results of various projects are delivered while a programme is underway
- Objectives and associated added value must not just be realized at the end of a programme, but also during the programme itself. These also fall within the responsibility of the programme
- The objectives of a programme often can not be achieved with the products and services delivered within one project. The results of several connected projects are generally required to achieve specific objectives. Nevertheless, the results of the individual projects can be essential for realizing the programme goals
- A programme has to be consciously closed. The decision must be made as to how long the benefits of maintaining a separate programme organization continue to justify the extra costs. There will come a moment when separate organization of the change management is no longer desirable via a programme, and that this is better returned to the business organization. The programme will then be closed, the programme organization dissolved, and discharge issued to respective personnel. The closing of a programme must thus be consciously determined and initiated. This contrasts with a project, where the end of the project automatically follows the completion of the project delivery.

Tension can sometimes occur between the pressure on projects to deliver the results on time and within budget and the need to realize the objectives as set out in the programme. The harmonization of these cannot be left to the individual project teams, but must be co-ordinated by programme management.

Project	Programme
• Include project activities	• Include project and business activities
• Co-ordinate work packages	• Co-ordinate projects
• Delivery product of service	• Realising objectives
• Ends by handing over output	• Must be closed formally
• Benefits accrue at end or after the project	• Benefits realised during Programme & afterwards
• Shorter timescale	• Longer timescale

Table. 3.1 Differences between Projects and Programmes

3.4 Multi-project management

Multi-project management involves managing a group of existing and future projects; the only thing these projects have in common is that they use the same staff and resources.

Projects are based on a client-supplier environment whereby the client supplies the actual results of the project and provides the necessary staff and resources. The client and the supplier can be part of the same or a different organization. Multi-project management is the responsibility of the business management within the supplier's organization.

- Within multi-project management, optimization of management, staff and resources for the independent projects involves the following important points:
- Development of a joint reporting structure and joint methods and techniques can lead to increased harmony between the projects and the business organization.
- Grouping of project-related activities within a business unit can ensure that other units can remain focused on their primary responsibilities
- Joint purchasing of products and services and/or joint hiring of staff can lead to economies of scale and professionalization of purchase and hire
- Setting-up a joint project office can lead to improved project support, both quantitative and qualitative
- Staff and resources can be deployed more efficiently through the use of 'pools'.

Without a joint objective, it is difficult to reach a rational decision regarding the allocation of staff and resources in individual projects. The projects with the most powerful sponsors and clients might start to dominate, without this being in the interests of the business organization.

Within a multi-project environment, projects also have a coherence that goes beyond use of the same staff and resources. Several projects are often carried out for the same client, thus leading to dependence, and they can be governed by the fact that they arise from a certain market or a certain skill that needs to be developed.

With multi-project management, it is possible to make use of methods and techniques such as those developed within programme management.

3.5 Portfolio management

Portfolio management involves managing a group of projects together, producing new capabilities that are necessary for realizing one or more joint goals.

As mentioned above, projects are based on a client-supplier environment. The client is the person or group placing the order to carry out the project and benefiting from the end result. Portfolio management is the responsibility of the client organization.

Various individual projects within the client organization that are at a disadvantage compared with a group of connected projects. Individual projects have a smaller chance than projects in a portfolio of being given sufficient consideration from senior management. This means there is less chance that the individual projects will fit in well with the goals of the business, compared with projects in a portfolio. The priority of projects is determined by being jointly managed from, on the one hand, the goals to be realized and the improvements required for this and, on the other hand, the available deployment of staff and resources. The various projects may deliver solitary or sometimes tranches of results, offering the organization the possibility of realizing its objectives.

The various projects are administered jointly within portfolio management, so the business or programme management can realize the added value. The total portfolio of projects in an organization can consist of various programmes, as well as project groups managed by senior management of the business units. The portfolio can also include maintenance and development projects falling under the responsibility of the various services within the business units. The individual portfolios should be managed separately within the programmes, the various business units and the individual services. Programmes can thus form part of the portfolios, and a portfolio will therefore be part of a programme.

3.6 A large project

A large project is not the same as a programme; there is a clear difference between the two terms. Programmes and large projects must thus be managed differently.

A large project seems a relative term. What one person understands by the term 'project' is common practice for the next person. For the management of projects, however, it is not important whether a project is a unique or common practice.

From a management point of view, a large project involves various sub-projects, each individually managed as a project. A large project often has more Project Boards on various levels within the project as a whole. It often runs longer than a 'normal' project and there are often more organizations involved in completing it. The composition of the parties can also change during the project.

A large project, however, remains one project; it realizes products and services. The Management of the project itself is not responsible for realizing either the goals or added value for the business organization.

It is essential to recognize these differences in establishing whether a project or a programme must be set-up. Everything relates to the choice of allocation of responsibilities and authorities of the individual parties. The temporary organization must be set-up accordingly; to a project model or a programme model.

For a large project, the methods and techniques of a programme can, of course, be used. The most significant difference remains that the management of a large project does not have to realize the goals of the business.

1 Projectmatig werken, Geert Grote, and others
2 De weg naar projectsucces, Teun van Aken
3 Project management, an introduction based on PRINCE2,, Fredriksz, and others
4 Nederlandse Competentie Baseline, PMI-Nederland

Principles of programme management

This part of the book describes the concepts, strategies, plans and techniques required for the co-ordinated organization, management and implementation of programmes. It is divided into:

- Organization and leadership

- Benefits management

- Stakeholder management and communication

- Risk- and issue resolution

- Programme planning- and management

- Business Case management

- Quality management

4 Organization and leadership

4.1 Introduction

Establishing good programme organization, with a clear and suitable description of everybody's tasks, responsibilities and authorities, is an essential condition for setting-up, leading and managing a programme and achieving the desired goals. The right people being in the right place with the right skills, attitude and behaviour is a pre-condition of good programme management.

Programmes are not stable. They are inconstant phenomena, highly susceptible to change, and highly dependent on the environment, changing visions and changes in course from the business organization of which they are a part. Strong leadership, a direct link between the programme and business management, a flexible management structure and an adequate decision-making process are therefore of considerable importance for a programme.

Programme management is most effective if issues and risks can be discussed openly and communication is a two-way process. This demands a leadership style and a company culture based on openness and clarity, with those concerned given the maximum opportunity to take responsibility for their own tasks.

4.2 Programme management: a choice

Programme management does not occur by itself, neither is it a 'must' in a given situation. Programme management is a choice; the Management of an organization can also legitimately decide not to choose a separate programme but to continue controlling the changes entirely from the normal line management activities.

In practice, there is often either a Management Team or the Management of an organization that struggles with a large number of changes to be carried out. A lot of management and meeting time can be lost in giving direction to and managing programmes, and the resulting changes, where large parts of the organization are involved and the programmes are repeated. If this is the case, it makes sense to place this 'time waster' outside the management meeting by making one of the Directorial or Management Team members responsible for managing the change along with his existing responsibilities.

Someone who advocated the particular change in the previous phase is often selected for this. Given the complexity of the change, it is clear that this managerially responsible person must be decisive and a *primus inter pares* within the Management or Directorial Team if this delegation is to succeed. It is as if a temporary matrix structure is placed over the existing responsibilities of business management.

For the duration of the programme, the person in question is ultimately responsible for the programme from the Board of Directors/Senior Management Team (SMT), and is the Senior Responsible Owner for all those concerned with the programme. As a capable manager, he does not carry out the work himself but appoints a Deputy Manager to provide daily management on his behalf for the setting-up and managing of the necessary changes. He will, however, remain managerially responsible for the final outcome.

Acting as Senior Responsible Owner does not change the fact that each Member of the Board/SMT remains responsible for his own department. From this function, he remains responsible for carrying out any alterations necessary for realizing the desired changes and providing the intended outcome. The Senior Responsible Owner cannot accept this; otherwise, he will accept responsibility from the other line managers. If this happens, it is a completely different management model. A new unit should be set-up to be responsible for the new business opportunity.

The other line managers will not carry out work connected with the forthcoming changes. This would place too much pressure on the management of normal business activities. They will also appoint Deputy Managers to prepare and carry out the required changes and ensure they deliver the desired outcome.

The solution leads to a structure between the Board/SMT and the programmes, which allows the existing organization to maintain space for its own activities and still have direct control and responsibility for carrying out the desired changes. We refer to this chosen structure as a programme.

A programme is therefore not a must, but a choice.

4.3 Basic principles of effective leadership

Effective leadership is indispensable for carrying out changes within an organization. Good management is not enough; someone must take the lead and give direction, instil enthusiasm and create the conditions necessary to actually carry out the changes. Here, leadership takes over from simple management.

Good leadership requires:
- Delegated decision-making: ensure individuals in the organization have sufficient authority to carry out the necessary decisions, but also find sufficient stimulation to be able to, and want to, take this on. This involves ensuring the competence of staff and that a suitable remuneration and assessment system exists to remove any blocks in work and decision-making processes
- Visible involvement and authority of the line managers in general, and particularly of the manager who has final responsibility, to such an extent that the parties concerned are motivated and the deployment of staff and resources can be guaranteed
- Finding a good balance between the necessary changes and the existing business management.
- Focus on the added value to be achieved for the organization and all parties individually concerned
- Relevant skills and experience to cope efficiently with the cultural and personal aspects of the changes: to solve problems with respect to the deployment of staff and resources, to harmonize programmes, and to manage uncertainty both within the programme and between the programme and the environment.

Periods of change carry a great risk factor if the added value of the changes does not benefit all parties concerned, or if the parties do not feel this is the case. (See chapter 18.)

4.4   Programme organization

The programme organization is the provisional organization set-up to achieve the programme, with defined roles and a consultative structure.

The Programme Management Team consists of the Senior Responsible Owner, the Programme Manager, the Business Change Managers, the Programme Office, any other supporting roles, the other Members of the Programme Board (optional) and the Sponsoring Group:

- *Sponsoring Group:* consists of all managers who have final responsibility for the business units involved in carrying out the strategic change. This Sponsoring Group can consist of all members of an SMT or Board of Directors, but might also be a partial gathering.
- *Senior Responsible Owner:* the person who is managerially and finally responsible to the Sponsoring Group. The Senior Responsible Owner is part of the Sponsoring Group and is preferably a *primus inter pares* within it.
- *Programme Manager:* is responsible for daily management of the programme under direct control of the Senior Responsible Owner.
- *Business Change Managers:* persons responsible for carrying out the changes and realizing the objectives in the individual business units.
- *Programme Office:* the organizational unit responsible for administrative and professional support of the programme.
- *Programme Board (optional):* a platform that can be set-up to help the Senior Responsible Owner to direct and control the programme (see figure 4.4. for an example).

Various projects and line activities are carried out as part of a programme. The projects have their own project organization, in addition to the above-described programme organization.

For a description of the tasks, responsibilities and authorities of the various roles and the skills required for carrying out these roles, see chapter 19.

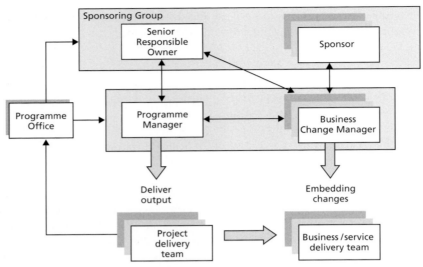

Fig. 4.1 Programme organization (© Crown copyright 2003 reproduced under licence from HMSO)

4.5 Sponsoring Group

The Sponsoring Group consists of all managers with final responsibility within the business units for realizing the programme's goal and achieving the associated added value. The Members of the Sponsoring Group are usually Members of the Management Team or the company's Board of Directors. It is the managers with final responsibility who must also authorize the change to be carried out. The realization of the change is actually doomed to fail without their active support.

The important point here is that Members of the Sponsoring Group not only approve the change, but that they are committed to it and also actively sell it to their own organization. In this context, their conduct is more important than that which they themselves endorse. Their daily activities must be guided by the envisaged changes; only then will their support to the changes be seen by third parties.

If their conduct should seem to be in conflict with the change to be implemented, they must actively explain why they are departing from standards, or state why the conduct is actually in line with the change. For example, if the organization has to make enormous savings and Management nevertheless decides to remain in its expensive premises, then they will have to explain why.

It could be that selling their premises and leasing a simpler property is very uneconomical in the current market situation, and that it is better to wait a few years. If so, this should be made clear.

As well as signing the new policy by the sponsors, it is also important for them to show leadership that supports the implementation of changes (see also paragraph 4.3), such as delegated decision-making, focus on added value, and so on. It is important within their own business units that a culture arises in which issues and uncertainties can be discussed openly and where communication is really a two-way concept.

The sponsors take the initiative to start the programmes. They appoint the person who will be managerially responsible for implementing the change (the Senior Responsible Owner), formulate the initial framework (Programme Mandate) and ask the Senior Responsible Owner to formulate a programme proposal (initiation phase). The Sponsoring Group must also approve the proposal and give the green light for beginning the programme. The Senior Responsible Owner then set-ups the Programme Definition (definition phase). This must be done in close consultation with the Sponsoring Group. It is important in this phase that the Sponsoring Group also remains the owner of the programme. The Sponsoring Group must officially assess and approve the Programme Definition, and give the go-ahead to commence implementation of the final programme (see figure 4.1).

During the programme, it is the sponsors who are finally responsible for the realization of the envisaged objectives for their own business units. They will have to address their own staff on this issue. On realizing the various levels within the programme, the Sponsoring Group has the responsibility of assessing the entire programme and ascertaining whether to go ahead with the next level and if so, in what manner. If agreed, the Sponsoring Group will authorize the Senior Responsible Owner to take over the implementation of the following level. On completion, the Sponsoring Group will officially discontinue the programme and the Senior Responsible Owner will discharge those concerned.

(P.S.: A Sponsor as being a member of the Sponsoring Group is not a separate role within the method MSP itself. Within the context of this book Sponsors are named separately to explain more easily their role and the role of the members of the Programme Management Team towards them.)

4.6   Senior Responsible Owner

The Senior Responsible Owner is the member of the Sponsoring Group with final responsibility for the programme. This is preferably an added task to his responsibilities within his own organization. The Senior Responsible Owner should be a *primus inter pares* within the Sponsoring Group and also one of those taking or bearing the initiative of the proposed changes. The Project Executive should be responsible for the primary business unit that must implement the major part of the changes.

The role of the Senior Responsible Owner is one of leader and standard-bearer. He must lead the way, initiate and facilitate changes and engage the most important stakeholders. He must also provide and maintain clear interpretation for the change.

The Senior Responsible Owner must put together a team that can give shape to the programme, co-ordinate the projects and activities, and effectively control and implement the changes. The role of the Senior Responsible Owner is often a part-time function, but essential for the success of the programme.

The Senior Responsible Owner is appointed from within the Sponsoring Group. It is not recommended that the Senior Responsible Owner be appointed from outside the Sponsoring Group, as he must own and be managerially responsible for the change, which would be difficult for an outside person.

Based on the Programme Mandate, the Senior Responsible Owner will first of all have to understand and set-up a plan for creating a more extensive Programme Definition. In the programme proposal, he will have to make an initial start on formulating a programme vision in a summary of the benefits to be achieved. The Sponsoring Group approves the programme proposal and appoints the Senior Responsible Owner based on this. They authorize the Programme Definition to be set-up under the responsibility of the Senior Responsible Owner, who will often make use of a small programming team to support him. The programme Vision Statement and the Blueprint for the changed organization will be coloured in, the approach to the implementation of the changes will be determined, and the management structure for the programme laid down. In this phase, there will be precise contact between the various members of the Sponsoring Group, and other stakeholders, with their own organization to be sure the programme will be supported by all parties. The Senior Responsible Owner is the owner of the Programme Definition.

During the implementation of the programme, the Senior Responsible Owner leads the programme and the Programme Team. He appoints the Programme Manager and ensures that the other programme roles are adequately filled. The Senior Responsible Owner will: advise the Programme Manager, supervise overall progress, give direction to the programme implementation, be responsible for solving possible bottlenecks, ensure the programme's goal continues to fit in with the company's changed goals, arrange support for the programme at the highest possible level, and be finally responsible for realizing the defined benefits. In his role as principal, he will review the programme during the transition from level to level. On completing the programme, the Senior Responsible Owner will be responsible for concluding activities and dissolving the programme organization.

4.7 Programme Manager

The Programme Manager is responsible for daily management of the programme and, in this function, reports directly to the Senior Responsible Owner. He is directly responsible for ensuring that new skills for implementing the changes become available, for reporting within the programme, and for communicating the programme to various stakeholders. The role demands starting and co-ordinating various projects, and agreeing the programme results with the Business Change Managers.

The Programme Manager can be someone from the organization itself or someone from outside. It is important that the Programme Manager possesses the correct skills and the drive to fulfil this role efficiently. As well as having management resources, knowledge and experience of programme management, the Programme Manager must also have strong communication skills and be capable of creating sufficient support with various stakeholders. The Senior Responsible Owner is finally responsible for the programme, but the Programme Manager carries the flag directly next to, or in front of him.

The Programme Manager is responsible for the correct context and balance in implementing the programme and must ensure that the final outcome is consistent with the policy frameworks applying in the organization. The Programme Manager is in charge of the Programme Office.

The Programme Manager is preferably appointed at the beginning of the definition phase and will sometimes be involved as early as the identification phase, whether or not he has already assumed the role of Programme Manager. At this stage, the programme has still not officially started. The Programme Manager must be appointed no later than the start of carrying out the programme. The choice of Programme Manager partly depends on the type of change to be implemented, which might be based on culture or more externally oriented such as increasing the market share. This determines which type of person is most suitable to fill the role of Programme Manager. The dominant strategy chosen for implementing the changes in the organization is also important for the choice of Programme Manager. It is also possible that one person is more suitable in the definition phase than in the implementation phase, in which case it is advisable that the Programme Manager be a member of the Programme Team. The choice of a Programme Manager is essential for the success of the programme, but it depends on the culture of the organization, the changes to be implemented, and the right person in the right place.

4.8 Business Change Managers

The Business Change Manager is mainly oriented towards realizing the benefits. He is also responsible for managing the added value within his own organization, which involves identifying possible benefits, implementing changes and realizing added value within his own department.

The Business Change Manager is appointed by the directly involved sponsor from the Sponsoring Group. The Senior Responsible Owner must ensure that an efficient Business Change Manager is appointed for each department involved or for each sponsor.

The sponsor is finally responsible for the changes being implemented in his own department and for realizing added value. The Business Change Manager is operationally responsible in this context. The Business Change Manager reports to his sponsor regarding the programme to the Senior Responsible Owner. In practice, the latter often takes place via the Programme Office.

The Business Change Manager is preferably chosen from his own department. The person in question must have experience within his own organization and production process. The Business Change Manager must be accepted by his own organization and have enough seniority to be able to implement the changes. He should possess management skills in order to work with and control people from various departments and sub-departments. The Business Change Manager must be oriented to realizing the benefits.

If more branches or departments come under the jurisdiction of one part of the company or one sponsor, it might be opportune to appoint more Business Change Managers within the overall department. For control purposes, it is much better for the sponsor to appoint one Business Change Manager with final responsibility in his department, including separate Business Change Managers below him for each business unit.

It is recommended that responsibility for the role of Business Change Manager fit in with the Business Change Manager's own responsibilities in daily work. The role of Business Change Manager is a part-time position. It is preferable that the Business Change Manager is not released from his normal work, but fulfils the role of Business Change Manager as well as his normal activities. The Business Change Manager is someone in the middle of business activities, often under pressure, and often asked for advice by colleagues and Management. The Business Change Manager must be the informal leader on the shop floor or the Crown Prince within a department. He often replaces the Manager of the organization during normal business. It is better to appoint and support a person like this, rather than someone with extra time but who is on the sidelines of production.

The Business Change Manager is responsible for identifying and quantifying the benefits in the definition phase. During implementation, the Business Change Manager must ensure the programme results are positive and are made available on time to be able to implement the changes adequately and on time within his own department. The Business Change Manager must secure the interest of his own department within the programme. Within his department, the Change Manager must ensure: that those concerned are open to changes, that the changes are feasible, are implemented with consideration to normal business activity, that added value is achieved and measured for the organization, and finally that 'business as usual' becomes his own organization's new method of working. On concluding the programme, the Business Change Manager must ensure continued improvement of the production process, and that continued measurement of the improvements is covered in the operational organization.

The Production Managers are responsible for production. They are the people who actually achieve the added value. The Business Change Manager must manage the process in order to generate extra added value in the organization. Only if the Business Change Manager is himself a Production Manager (or one of them), will he be responsible for realizing some of the agreed added value.

4.9   Programme Office

A Programme Office is an organizational unit responsible for administrative and professional support of the programme. Most programmes have their own Programme Office, but there may be a joint Programme Office within an organization that supports other programmes at the same time.

The tasks and authorities of a Programme Office can vary considerably. Within some programmes, the Programme Office has mainly administrative tasks, such as registering and distributing documents, change management and timekeeping. Other Programme Offices are more oriented towards managing the programme, and registering and reporting on progress in realizing the benefits, with a type of 'dashboard' directed towards the various critical performance indicators (KPIs) to be achieved.

Programme Offices often provide more professional support, such as planning and budget monitoring, arranging purchasing and seconding, programme assurance and holding reviews and audits. They also sometimes have an advisory role in drafting the overall programme and in the Blueprint for the new organization.

The Programme Office is sometimes combined with individual projects' Project Support Offices. The advantage of this is that deployment of staff and resources can be divided up and that joint expertise can be consolidated, which guarantees that information between projects is unequivocal and consistent. A disadvantage can be that the Programme Office is oriented too much towards producing the necessary results and too little on achieving the agreed added value.

The Programme Office is set-up immediately on receiving the green light for implementing the programme. The members of the Programme Office are appointed by the Programme Manager in consultation with the Senior Responsible Owner. The Programme Office then arranges the setting-up of the necessary procedures and infrastructure for the programme. The Programme Office is run by the Programme Manager, with the Deputy Programme Manager often the Head of the Programme Office.

4.10 Setting-up the programme organization

Programme organization can be set-up on a one-off basis or be part of a continued series in an organization. Programmes can be set-up in a 'lean and mean' manner or, broadly speaking, with several supporting services. Programmes may include one or just a few main projects parallel to a few small programmes, or might include a few hundred projects spread across various branches or even different countries. Programmes may come entirely within an organization or arise from co-operation between various organizations.

No two programmes are the same. This is why a specific programme organization will have to be designed for each programme, to fit in with the complexity of the environment, the end goal to be achieved, the urgency of the change, the organization's terms of reference and culture, and the individual players in the field.

Within a Programme Management Team, it can be desirable to set-up a Programme Board consisting of the most important stakeholders, partners and investors who support the Senior Responsible Owner in directing and controlling the programme. The Senior Responsible Owner will preferably chair such a Programme Board.

In many programmes, a separate platform will also be set-up in which the Senior Responsible Owner, the Programme Manager and the various Business Change Managers consult as to controlling the programme. This is typically the platform on which the operational bottlenecks and uncertainties within the programme are managed. The Senior Responsible Owner preferably chairs this consultation, but if he only takes part in the consultation occasionally, the Programme Manager will chair the discussions.

4.11 Integrating programmes and projects

Programmes and projects normally have their own organization. It can, however, be beneficial to have part of the programme and project organization overlap (see figure 4.2).

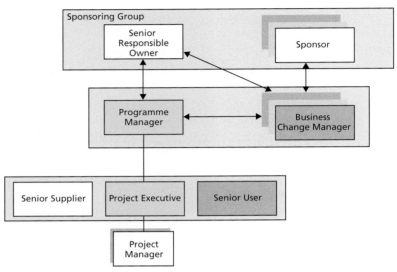

Fig. 4.2 Integration of project and programme roles

The Programme Manager can fulfil the role of the Project Executive. This can be desirable for a project within a programme to ensure a direct link between the project and the programme. From the role as Project Executive, he is the 'owner' of the problem within the programme and responsible for ensuring the Business Case, fitting the project into the programme and finding the balance between the interests of the users and executives/suppliers. This role fits in well with his role within the programme, where, as Programme Manager, he is responsible for co-ordinating the projects and tuning the projects to the programme.

The role of the Senior User in a programme can be carried out by one of the Business Change Managers. From his role as Senior User, he will be responsible within the programme for: delivering the requirements, providing the necessary staff and resources from the users' organizations, having the programme results assessed, approving the changes and representing the interests of the users within the programme generally. As Senior User, he will represent all the users' groups and be responsible for communication with the parties regarding the programme. This role fits in well with his role as Business Change Manager, where he is responsible for ensuring that the programme delivers what is necessary to realize the agreed added value for his own organization.

The various projects within a programme can be controlled by a Central Board instead of separate Boards for individual projects. In this case, various Project Managers will report to the same Board. The most logical thing is for the Programme Manager to chair the Central Programme Board and for one or more Business Change Managers to fulfil the role of Senior User. A brainstorming group might be used if there are several Business Change Managers, as this can considerably shorten the lines and significantly improve effectiveness of control.

Such constructions also have advantages in the efficiency of staff deployment. However, the disadvantage is that responsibilities are heaped up and, as the circle of people involved in the programme is limited, this can cause support problems. The rest of the organization will see the problem as relating only to a limited group, which is a real danger.

4.12 Division of roles

Just as roles can be grouped, they can also be divided up among various people in a programme (see figure 4.3). This can be particularly necessary or desirable within big programmes, those requiring diverging expertise, or those spread over several locations.

The Programme Manager might be supported in his role by a Risk Manager, Design Architect or Purchasing Manager. He is also sometimes supported by a Financial Manager or Controller. These roles can be filled from the Programme Office or separately. The latter will particularly apply if separate organizational units within his own organization already exist for these roles and support is arranged from these units.

In addition to the Business Change Manager, a Co-ordinating Business Change Manager is often appointed, who consults directly with the Programme Manager and also controls other Business Change Managers. This is particularly the case if several locations or organizational units are involved, where their own changes are to be implemented and benefits realized within each unit or location; for example, a representation from an employer's organization, if measures need to be implemented for a large number of areas of the businesses.

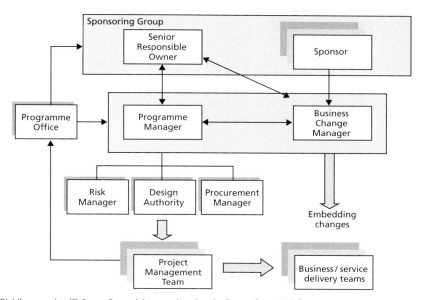

Fig. 4.3 Dividing up roles (© Crown Copyright reproduced under licence from HMSO)

4.13 Programmes in serveral organizations

Programmes are often implemented involving several organizations at the same time and in such a way that they fulfil certain joint objectives, which could not be achieved so well without one another (see figure 4.4).

A well-known example is, of course, the setting-up of private/public co-operatives between governments and private companies. This could involve, for example, neighbourhood development where residential housing associations and property developers are in association with the local authority. Without good co-operation, the objectives of the individual parties would be hardly or not at all realizable.

The Sponsoring Group consists of various parties that agree to achieve certain objectives together. A Programme Board is formed from the Sponsoring Group with managerial representatives from the various parties and from which the Senior Responsible Owner is appointed. The Senior Responsible Owner chairs the Programme Board and is preferably the managerial representative of the most dominant sponsor in the co-operative.

In such a co-operation, it it of considerable importance to have mutual trust and respect, recognition of each other's interests and positions, the various parties' expertise, and the leadership of the Senior Responsible Owner and other members of the Programme Board.

They must also emphatically support the Senior Responsible Owner's leadership.

Another essential factor is that the necessity of the co-operation and the change to be implemented are clear for all parties, both for sponsors and other stakeholders in the programme. It must always be clear why the change is to be implemented and what will go wrong if this is not done.

The roles for all parties must be clear for all concerned, as well as who will bear which costs and risks. In the event of overspending, consideration must be paid to the management model for what to do and who bears the extra expense.

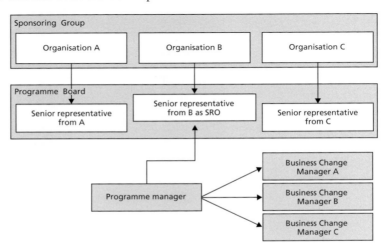

Fig. 4.4 Multi-organizational programmes (© Crown copyright 2003 reproduced under licence from HMSO)

The points of authorization must be agreed clearly in advance. The process model is important: at which stages do we wish to achieve something, what should be clear, to what level of detail and how will decision-making take place? The added value of separate parties must be clear to continue the co-operation. This requires more control than in a normal programme.

4.14   HRM aspects in programmes

Human Resource Management is crucial in a programme. Management cannot expect everything to start work by itself, just by a programme being announced. What is most important is having the right person in the right place. It can be like looking for a rare four-leaf clover; there is not much chance that somebody will be suitable for all aspects of a role within a programme. Much consideration should be given to training people, developing the necessary skills and also to creating teams.

Besides those directly involved in a programme, consideration must also be given to middle management and other line managers in the organization. Programmes lay a matrix structure over the organization, altering the tasks, responsibilities and authorities of the other managers. Are they aware of this, are they prepared for it, and is it seen to be so?

This also changes for the staff involved in the programmes. Firstly, they now get two bosses. They may already be used to working on programmes, but this may be new for them. Staff involved should not be entirely relieved from their daily work, but continue this in parallel with programme tasks. This will bind staff to the company, and draw a little more on their goodwill. However, carrying out programme work in the evening as a consequence of this should be avoided.

Staff must be partly relieved from their daily work, with support provided for the other part of the programme work. Do staff and managers realize this and is it planned for? The assessment and remuneration structure must take this into account, and agreements must be made on the consequences of working in the programme for an individual's career prospects. If this is not done sufficiently, the programme will run aground before it has even started.

5   Benefits management

5.1   Introduction

The benefits: this is where it all started. Every programme starts with a vision, a dream of a better future. Whether the goal is solving or preventing a problem, or extending chances in the future, each change involves realizing benefits. It is the added value that makes it wise to invest in new things and in changes.

A programme basically entails enablers that deliver results, which deliver new or improved capabilities for the organization when the business organization actually starts working with these. Management can use these new or improved capabilities to achieve its goals and reap all the benefits. Positive or negative side effects might occur when realizing the secondary goals. The changed situation enables the organization to really work differently and realize the envisaged benefits. The programme has achieved the end goal if the organization has adopted this new manner of working and realized the goals and associated benefits (see figure 5.1).

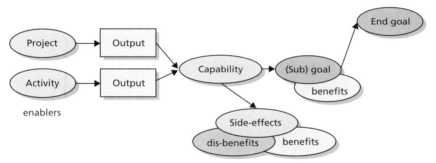

Fig. 5.1 Set-up of realization of benefits due to change

A programme is ultimately about realizing the benefits. Benefits management is a fundamental aspect of running a programme. It is a continuous activity that carries on even after the end of the programme. Benefits management ensures the benefits are identified, monitored and measured. It creates the link between the benefits and the secondary goals of the programme and can also help stimulate involvement and create managerial ownership.

Benefits management helps the Programme Management Team to maintain the focus on realizing the benefits as well as realizing the necessary capabilities.
  The goals of benefits management are to ensure that:
- All benefits have been identified and defined, and relate to the strategic goals of the programme
- All the business units involved are committed to the benefits and their realization
- The business organizations become the owners of the benefits and realize the benefits via their business management
- There is proactive management and measurement of the benefits (also baseline measurement)
- The formulated benefits are challenging but realistic
- Direction is given to the programme and ensuring the benefits are delivered in line with the business goals and the business strategy

- The benefits are realized, measured and established, as well as recognized and appreciated
- The benefits fit in with the vision and the desired outcome of the programme.

5.2 Benefits management process

The benefits management process is closely related to the Business Case and Business Case Management. The Business Case is the practical justification for the programme. It compares the costs and consequences of the change with the advantages and output that must be achieved following the change. Here, the balance between advantages/costs and advantages/output must justify entering into the costs and the risks of the change.

Benefits management activities are seen in the benefits management process, which gives structure to all the activities necessary to optimize realization of the benefits from the beginning of the programme (see figure 5.2).

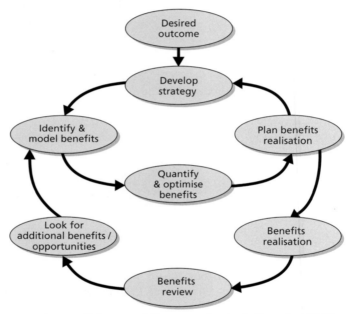

Fig 5.2 Benefits management process (© Crown copyright 2003 reproduced under licence from HMSO)

5.3 Benefits management strategy

A benefits management strategy is based on the secondary goals, and states who is to realize and measure the goals. This strategy provides the Programme Management Team with a structure for realizing the objectives of the programme and is therefore crucial to it.

It is important that the strategy coincides with the programme goals, the culture of the organization, the changes to be carried out and the standards of the business organization. A central policy agreement must be implemented for dealing with benefits management, so that everyone works in the same manner. In this way, the strategy is clear, interchangeable and manageable. Furthermore, the strategy must be agreed with the Blueprint in order to match the benefits with the realization of capabilities. The benefits management strategy must be adjusted regularly, at least at the end of each cluster of projects.

The benefits management strategy describes in detail how and to what extent the benefits are quantified, the measuring means to be used, and who is responsible for realizing the various secondary goals and their associated benefits. Bearing in mind that the strategy contains a division of responsibilities, it is important to ensure that those involved have knowledge of the plan and are behind it. The benefits must be realized in and by the business organization; this makes involvement by the stakeholders an important aspect of developing the benefits management strategy.

Make choosing the best benefits management strategy a joint priority!

The following aspects of a benefits management strategy must be tested:
- Does the total of the benefits fit in with what is expected of the programme?
- Have the relevant stakeholders been sufficiently involved in developing the strategy?
- Does the organization have enough capacity and capabilities to realize the strategy?
- Have the people who will be finally responsible for realizing the benefits been identified, have agreements been made with them on this, and are they committed to carrying these out?
- Has the benefits management strategy been integrated into other plans and strategies in the programme?

5.4 Identifying the benefits

The process of identifying the benefits is the first step in establishing the vision and the goals to be realized via the programme. This takes place on a relatively general level; the benefits then become more concrete during the process of defining the programme. Benefits can transpire in several different fields (see table 5.1).

Category	Description
Economics	Benefits of saving costs without affecting product quality
Internal management	Benefits for the internal organization such as improving quality and decision-making
Quality of services	Benefits for clients such as faster and/or more adequate services or improved provision of information
Organizational flexibility	Benefits of increasing the organization's ability to react to changing circumstances
Strategic support	Benefits contributing to the realization of other advantages or initiatives being developed within the organization
Increasing employee motivation	An often indirect benefit forming the basis for other benefits, i.e., reducing sickness absenteeism, increasing flexibility, productivity and innovative involvement
Increased productivity	Benefits enabling the organization to carry out the same task with fewer staff or resources enabling a reduction of production costs
Reducing risk	A benefit of better preparation of the organization for the future, for example, by reducing dependence on one supplier, preventing disruption to the production process or reducing seasonal dependence in the sale of products
Obligations	Demands, for example, laid down by the Government
Increasing profit	Benefits contributing to an organization's increased net profits or speeding up the profits

Table 5.1 Various categories of benefits

A outcome relationship model can be used to get a good picture of the total outcomes and benefits. This diagram gives an overview of all (secondary) outcomes and the relations between them. Figure 5.3 is an example of such a model.

The relationships between the outcomes play an important role in determining the priorities for the programme activities.

Of course, it would be nice if a programme only had advantages, but disadvantages can often be found too. One person's improvement can be disadvantageous for the next person. There might be benefits to be had, but these could lead to a problem or extra expense elsewhere. This is referred to as a 'dis-benefit' or a negative benefit. It is necessary to ensure that the consequences of disadvantages do not become too significant for the programme. The dis-benefits must be considered when setting-up the Business Case. Setting out possible disadvantages is therefore an important aspect of Benefits Management.

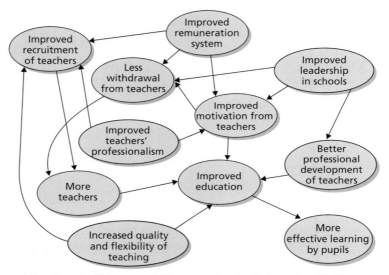

Fig. 5.3 Outcome relationship model (© Crown copyright 2003 reproduced under licence from HMSO)

It is important that each benefit is linked to an owner who is responsible to senior management for realizing the benefits. The Senior Responsible Owner has responsibility for all the benefits within the programme. A good way of ensuring ownership of the benefits is to include them in the Business Score Cards of the various business units and link them to the performance bonuses of individual staff.

5.5   Quantifying the benefits

We stated earlier that quantifying the benefits is important for measuring and managing them. But how are benefits realized in concrete terms? And how can this be measured? Benefits can be classified as indirect, direct non-financial or direct financial benefits (see figure 5.4).

With more financial value, it can be quite simple to quantify and measure the benefits. It is also reasonably easy to show increases in productivity. However, it can sometimes be very difficult to make a precise assessment in the case of indirect benefits as to what these will be in the future. It sometimes appears that benefits can only be described in general terms. Think about 'being more customer-friendly'. The question here is: what does it involve? Improving customer-friendliness can mean, for example, answering the telephone with "Good morning, my name is …" instead of "hello", or that complaints don't do the rounds within the organization but are dealt with in one location and are handled quicker. In such cases, a critical performance indicator (KPI) could be: the duration between the time when a complaint is registered up to it being concluded. Another method of measuring customer satisfaction is carrying out a customer satisfaction survey whereby clients are approached and asked to rate the service levels provided by the organization.

Critical performance indicators or key performance indicators (KPIs) must be determined, and it should be established how these are to be measured and what the current status is. If necessary, a 'baseline measurement' will have to be carried out first. Only then can a standard be set-up both for the desired final value and any intermediate values required; and only then is it possible to see, based on intermediate measurements during the programme, whether the objectives set are actually being achieved.

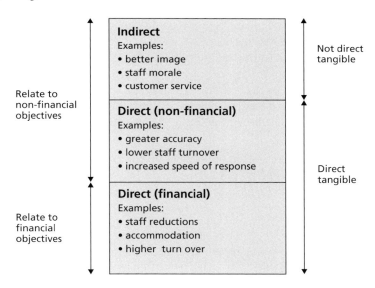

Fig, 5.4: Breakdown of the benefits

It is better to find out later that no good assumptions have been made, than to get no indication at all. Standards are not possible without indications, and without a standard, it is not possible to show whether the programme is successful or not.

When measuring benefits: quantify it, if necessary with assumptions!

The number of benefit types is so diverse that a whole series of measuring instruments might be required. The 'Earned Value' method can be used if this involves quantitative numbers. This system was originally introduced by the US Defense Department, and the key is the relation between the expected results and the results actually achieved in order to forecast the final result.

5.6 Benefits Profiles

A benefits profile must be set-up for each benefit. Whereas at the start we referred to general, guiding advantages, the benefits in the benefits profiles must now be clearly described and quantified. From 'working in a more client-oriented manner' to 'customer satisfaction of our major accounts must improve by 15% for subsidiary X'.

The benefits profile provides an overview of all relevant information on the benefits. The dis-benefits are also described and laid out in this way. The benefits profile for each benefit shows:
• The description of the benefits
• Dependencies on other benefits
• When the benefits will be realized and within what period of time
• The unit the benefits are expressed in, how this is to be measured, and the baseline measurement
• The financial contribution
• The necessary changes in the business management in order to realize the benefits
• Costs of realizing and measuring the benefits
• Dependencies of other projects, risks and programmes
• Project(s) directly related to realizing the benefits
• Those responsible for realizing the benefits
• The KPIs in the business management that are influenced by the benefits, with the current value of these KPIs and their value after realizing the benefits.

With a benefits profile, it is also possible to see whether the benefits are being carried out according to plan, as progress monitoring is possible. The Business Change Managers are often responsible for realizing the benefits.

A benefits profile for a programme is similar to a product description in a project. The realization of these benefits is the purpose of the programme. A clear and unambiguous description of the benefits provides focus about what must be implemented and when, and clarity as to when the agreed benefits have been realized.

5.7 Goals chart

The goals chart is used to make the link between the end goal and the required enablers. The end goal is divided into secondary goals, and these are divided into sub-secondary goals and finally into the necessary capabilities. The capabilities are again linked to the necessary results of projects and activities (see figure 5.5).

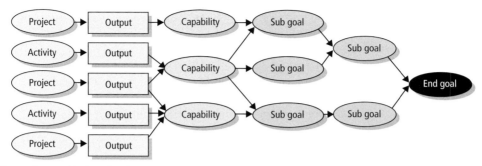

Fig. 5.5 From enabler to end goal

Setting-up such a goals chart ensures that all results are linked to the (secondary) goals. Filling in the chart can also be a reason for identifying new objectives.

The goals chart can be used at various levels: strategic level, plan level and result level[5] (see figure 5.6). On the strategic (or framework) level, goals are included for the long term; these can be programme goals. The acronym 'MACIM' is used for describing goals. It stands for Measurable, Acceptable (because it is realistic), Communicated (with those involved), Inspiring and Motivating. The lowest level is the result level, in which the required enablers are listed. The enablers must be described using the term SMART: Specific, Measurable, Acceptable, Relevant and Time-related.

5.8 Prioritizing

The goal within a programme is achieved by realizing various secondary goals, and delivering various projects and activities with the associated results. With an insight into the goals and the link with the enablers and capabilities, the Programme Management Team is in a position to set priorities. It is then known how a certain outcome contributes to a certain goal. This way, changes can provide a good picture as to the consequences, and Project Portfolio decisions will be easier.

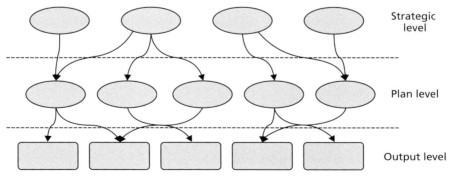

Fig. 5.6 Example of a goals chart

For prioritizing activities, it is necessary to set-up a number of criteria on which the projects are assessed. Preparing a logical sequence in the projects based on preconditions or start and finish times is often not enough. Many models have therefore been developed for prioritizing projects further, such as the Parker[6] model and the THEFD model[7]. Obviously, projects satisfying the legal framework must always be implemented.

5.8.1 The Parker model

In the Parker model, projects are mutually prioritized based on a number of qualitative and quantitative factors:
- *Return on investment:* the level with which the project yields results for the organization.
- *Strategic fit:* the level with which the project fits in with the organization's business plans and business strategies.
- *Competition advantages:* the level with which the project makes a contribution to the department's competitive position.
- *Competition pressure:* the level of importance in implementing a project from a competition point of view.
- *Management information:* the level with which the project supports Management in governing operational, tactical and strategic objectives.
- *Project and organizational risks:* the level with which success of the product depends on changes within the organization.
- *Infrastructure fit:* the level with which the project fits in with the future infrastructure.
- *Uncertainty of the outcome:* the level of uncertainty regarding how a certain end product should appear.
- *Technical risk:* the level to which sufficient technical knowledge and information are available for realizing the project.
- *Operational risk:* the level of uncertainty regarding maintenance and management of the products to be delivered.

For each assessment aspect, evaluation criteria are set-up which can be adjusted to the individual circumstances. It is then assessed via a multi-criteria analysis to see which projects within the programme can best be started.

5.8.2 The THEFD model

The THEFD model gives an overview of an assessment of projects and activities, and assumes five general criteria:
- *Speed*: which outcome contributes to the goal the fastest
- *Feasibility:* which outcome is most feasible (technically, financially or socially)
- *Efficiency:* which outcome is realized with the most efficient use of available means
- *Flexibility:* the realization of which results is easiest to stop, change or speed up
- *Goal-orientation:* which results contribute most to achieving the goals

The assessments of the projects and activities based on these criteria are processed in a priority matrix. As with the Parker method, it is then assessed via a multi-criteria analysis to see which projects within the programme can best be started (see table 5.2).

	Goal oriented	Effectiviness	Flexibility	Feasibility	Speed
Project A	4	2	4	3	2
Project B	1	3	2	2	1
Activity C	2	1	1	3	4
. . . . .					
Project N	3	3	2	3	3

Table 5.2 Priority matrix based on a scale of 1 to 5

5.9 Benefits realization plan

Results are delivered in the programme by the projects and activities, which together enable the change in the business organization. Within the programme, the Business Change Manager is supported in implementing the change. The change must become 'business as usual', and from the changed situation, the benefits can be realized by way of the primary processes. This forms the basis of programme management.

The benefits of change in the future should not be compared with the current state of affairs, but with the possible future state if no programme is set-up (the 'what if' scenario). The situation might be much worse than it is now because all sorts of negative developments might occur without the positive effect of the programme changes (see figure 5.7).

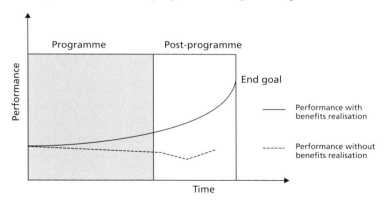

Fig. 5.7 Benefit realization diagram (© Crown copyright 2003 reproduced under licence from HMSO)

The Benefits Realization Plan helps co-ordinate the realization of the benefits and consists of a complete overview of all benefits profiles shown in a plan form. The planning states, among other things, when a benefit is to be realized and the points on which benefit realization assessments are maintained (see figure 5.8).

The Benefits Realization Plan is developed at the same time as the Programme Plan and the Business Case, to make sure that these are consistent. This creates the link between the results, the benefits and the Business Case. It can even be a good idea to combine the Programme Plan and the Benefits Realization Plan into one document.

It is often the case that not all the possible benefits are realized during the programme and the transfer of the programme to the permanent organization has to be arranged. Programmes are often dissolved before all the benefits have been realized, either because it is more efficient to govern the remaining improvements from the business organization, or because priority has been placed on other or new programmes.

In order to use the benefits as efficiently as possible, it is important to also consider the human aspects of changes. Realization of the benefits depends on the willingness of the organization to welcome the changed situation as its own. Good preparation and a sufficient introductory period will increase the chances of acceptance and the willingness and involvement of stakeholders.

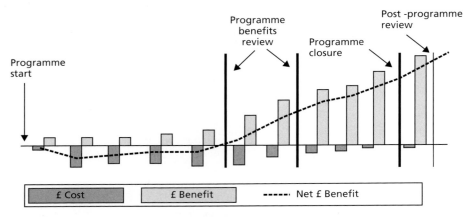

Fig. 5.8 Benefit realization within the time frame (© Crown copyright 2003 reproduced under licence from HMSO)

5.10 Review of benefits realization

We have often said: "It's all about the benefits!". Programmes are very intensive phases that have great impact on the organization concerned. Whether seen from the perspective of the user, changer or the client, programmes are visible elements in- and outside the organization. The costs of such a phase are often high, as are the risks involved. It may be like working towards an attractive vision, but what is the alternative?

It is therefore very important to return to the entire organization each time, and to bring this out into the open. By way of benefit realization assessments, a picture can be formed of the status of objectives already achieved. This is important for all stakeholders, and it is the stakeholders in the business organization who provide input for the assessment. It is the managers in the business organization who are in a position to give a realistic outline as to the progress and the effect.

In order to avoid a conflict of interest, it is important not to have the benefit realization assessments carried out by those directly involved.

The benefits realization consists of:
• Assessing and amending the benefits profiles and the Benefits Realization Plan
• Checking to see if the benefits still fit in with the programme goals
• Identifying new benefits
• Assessing the performance of the changed business organization

- Informing the stakeholders as to the progress
- Assessing the effectiveness of Benefits Management (evaluation).

5.11 Responsibilities

The Programme Management Team is responsible for Benefits Management and the Programme Manager is owner of the Benefits Realization Plan. The Business Change Managers are responsible for identifying and quantifying the benefits and are owners of the benefits profiles. The Project Management Teams support the Business Change Managers in identifying and quantifying the benefits and planning the benefits realization. The Programme Office monitors and reports on the progress of benefits realization. The benefits are realized by business management, although the Senior Responsible Owner remains finally responsible for realizing the benefits.

For an overview of the responsibilities of Benefits Management, see table 5.3.

Role	Responsibilities
Senior Responsible Owner	Owner of the benefits management strategy
	Delivers input and finally approves the benefits to be approved
	Delivers input and finally approves the Benefits Realization Plan
	Is in charge of benefits assessments
Programme Manager	Setting-up and implementing the benefits management strategy
	Owner of the benefits realization plan
Business Change Manager	Supporting the Programme Manager in setting-up and implementing the benefits management strategy
	Identifying and quantifying the benefits together with the stakeholders, PrgM and PMTs
	Owner of the benefits profiles
	Planning benefits realization together with PrgM and PMTs
	Realizes the benefits as part of the business organization
Programme Office	Monitors and reports the progress of the benefits organization
	Provides information for the benefits assessments
Business organization	Realizes the benefits

Table 5.3 Responsibilities within benefits realization

---

5 Projecten Leiden, Geert Groote and others
6 Information Economics, M.M. Parker and others
7 Programme management, Sturen op samenhang, G. Wijnen and others

6 Stakeholder management and communication

6.1 Introduction

Stakeholder management and communication are two of the most important aspects of any change. Changes always involve people and always have an impact on the people involved, no matter how technical the changes might seem.

A new ICT platform could create many other problems. The decision-makers should realize that older employees might have more difficulties with modern technology. The youngsters in the department might now be able to do more than the experienced old codgers, and this can sometimes upset relations within the department. Relations, including those involving positions of power, might change.

When anything changes, people tend to ask "What does it mean for me and will I be wiser for it?". It therefore follows that most people are naturally adverse to change and shy away from the unknown. Furthermore, if these people are not involved in the change, they will normally be against it from the beginning, the 'not-invented-by-us' scenario.

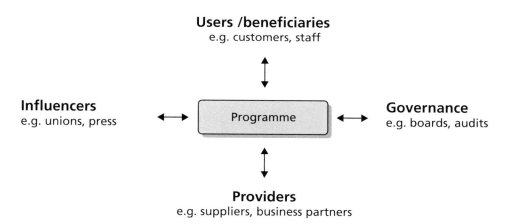

Fig. 6.1 Stakeholder influences (© Crown copyright 2003 reproduced under licence from HMSO)

All sorts of stakeholders must be taken into account, including the users, clients and supervisory parties, and those carrying out the activities and projects (see figure 6.1). This is the reason for keeping stakeholder management and communication high on any programme's agenda.

6.2 Stakeholder Management Strategy

Consideration must be given early in the programme to the Stakeholder Management Strategy: who are the stakeholders, what are their interests, what influence do they have, how should they be involved in the programme, what information do they need and how can they exercise influence within the programme?

It is essential that these aspects have already been considered in the identification phase. A plan must then be set-up for the definition phase: which team will set-up the Programme Definition, who will be involved, at which stages will this take place, who will approve the various documents and how much time and budget are available. Should the Works Council and/or the trade unions be involved and if so how? The plan must also be set-up from the point of view of the Stakeholder Management Strategy. The foundations for success (or failure) of the entire programme, including communication, are laid in the definition phase.

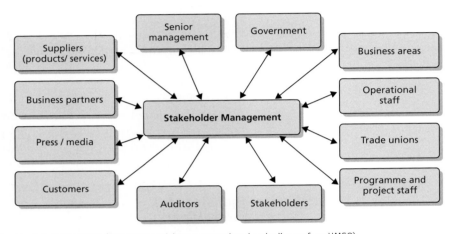

Fig.6.2 Possible Stakeholders (© Crown copyright 2003 reproduced under licence from HMSO)

An analysis of possible stakeholders is made in the definition phase (see figure 6.2), and an overview of stakeholders is drawn up. A Stakeholder Management Strategy and a Communication Plan should be worked out and established.

The Stakeholder Management Strategy is heavily dependent on:
• The level with which cultural, organizational and/or social changes must be implemented within the programme
• The level with which expectations must be managed
• The necessity for stakeholders to commit to the programme
• The level with which Management must also become owners of the programme
• The necessity for the goals and benefits to be communicated clearly and unambiguously.

The steps in a Stakeholder Management Strategy are:
• Analysis of the stakeholders
• Establishing the areas of interest of the various stakeholders
• Identifying the objectives of stakeholder management
• Ascertaining how the stakeholders are to be involved in the programme and how their feedback is to be processed
• Deciding how effectiveness of communication during implementation is tested.

6.3   Analysis of stakeholders

When analysing stakeholders, it is important to know who they are, the relationship between them, and their influence, interests and attitudes towards the programme. Such an analysis is often divided into the following steps:
- Listing the stakeholders
- Preparing a diagram showing relations between the parties involved
- Listing interests and influence
- Evaluating relations.

6.3.1 Listing the stakeholders

First, it is important to prepare a list of all stakeholders. See figure 6.3 for a summary of possible stakeholders when setting-up and implementing a programme. The list should include those parties directly, visibly and remotely involved. Such a list is often divided up into users, decision-makers, executives and suppliers.

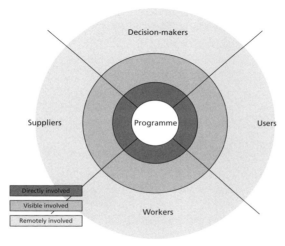

Fig. 6.3 List of stakeholders

The term 'users' includes all persons directly or indirectly involved with the final outcome. This includes direct users and Management of the departments involved, their internal and external clients, Management and Maintenance staff, and all those benefiting or burdened by the outcome or its realization.

6.3.2 Preparing a diagram showing relations between parties involved

After establishing who the stakeholders are, it is important to clarify the relations between the stakeholders. This is normally done with a diagram showing relations between the parties involved (see figure 6.4). This shows the relations between the most important stakeholders from the previous list by way of thicker or thinner lines; the thicker the line, the stronger the relation. Arrows can show how the relations are oriented.

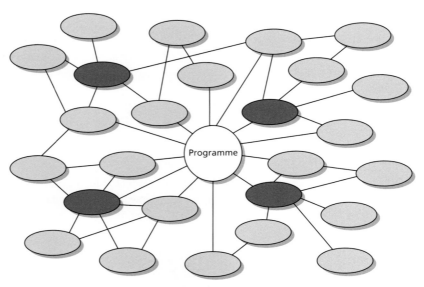

Fig. 6.4 Diagram showing relations between parties involved

This diagram makes it easy to establish which stakeholders are the 'spiders in the web'. It is important to be able to recognize these stakeholders, and to take special account of this when working on the Stakeholder Management Strategy.

6.3.3 Listing interests and influence

Based on the above diagram, a list can be drawn up of the interests and influence of the various stakeholders. This normally involves a diagram with the level of stakeholders' influence on the programme on one side, and their level of interest on the other (see figure 6.5). Is this interest positive, neutral of negative? The further apart from the middle line, the greater the interest is either positive or negative.

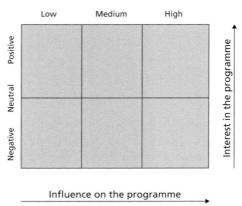

Fig. 6.5 Stakeholder-influence analysis

6.3.4 Evaluating relations

Based on the interest-influence analysis, it is possible to determine the relations between the stakeholder and the programme, whether these are positive or negative, and whether there is much or little confidence in the relations.

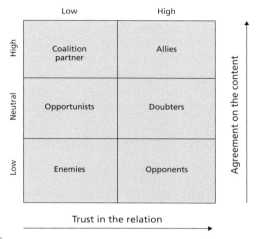

Fig. 6.6 Stakeholder attitudes

There are six basic relationships derived from these two variables (see figure 6.6):
- *Coalition partners:* there is a high level of agreement as to content but little confidence in the relations. You work well together but only after the form and content have been negotiated.
- *Allies:* there is a high level of agreement as to content and confidence in the relations. They often support one another through thick and thin, based on years of working together.
- *Opportunists:* there is a lack of clarity as to content. The opportunist also has little confidence in the relations. The basic attitude is one of "What's in it for me?"
- *Doubters:* there is a lack of clarity as to content. The doubter does, however, have a lot of confidence in the relations. Their standpoint is also unclear but they are open to discussion on this. The basic attitude is positive.
- *Adversaries:* they do not agree with the content and have little confidence in the relations. The relations are often emotional, determined by experience from the past with the same persons or the same situations.
- *Opponents:* they do not agree as to content but there is confidence in the relations. There is mutual respect for the other party.

Note: Relations can be other than estimated and might change in the course of the programme.

6.4   Stakeholders' areas of interest

After analysing the stakeholders, it is possible to ascertain their various interests. This is a rough indication of areas of interest for governing future communication. A summary of stakeholders is generally drawn up for such lists (see figure 6.7), which shows the various stakeholders with their respective areas of interest. These must be defined as accurately as possible, despite the simplicity of the summary.

Stakeholders	Reduced Costs	Better Performance	Better Flexibility	Reduced Risk	Greater Efficiency	Long Term Stability	Public Esteem	Competitive Advantage
Board	✓	✓	✓	✓	✓	✓	✓	✓
Executive	✓	✓	✓	✓	✓	✓	✓	✓
Managers				✓	✓	✓	✓	
Staff				✓		✓	✓	
Customers	✓		✓	✓	✓	✓	✓	
Community				✓		✓	✓	
Suppliers				✓		✓		
Unions				✓		✓		

Figure 6.7 Example of a Stakeholder Map

6.5 Objectives of stakeholder management

Part of Stakeholder Management Strategy is establishing which information stakeholders need and how feedback is processed from the stakeholders in the programme.

In order to establish this, it must first be clear what has to be achieved through communication. Communication should promote the realization and maximization of benefits, and support realization of the final programme goal. Based on this, the goals of stakeholder management can be described as:

- Ensuring the need for change remains clear
- Promoting co-operation and agreement
- Preventing unexpected intervention
- Maximizing identification of benefits
- Promoting involvement and commitment
- Ensuring expectations do not shift uncontrollably
- Ensuring everyone is heading in the same direction.

From this can be derived what has to be communicated and how. It is important to continuously emphasize the end goal of the programme, why this must be achieved and what the added value is. It is more effective to state what the desired final situation is, than to go over all sorts of plans about who has to do what and when. Antoine de Saint-Exupery says: "If you want to build a ship, don't bring people together to collect wood, prepare plans, make drawings and assign tasks but teach people how to long for the sea."

Show that management has embraced the latest developments, not only in word but also in deed. Ensure that everyone knows what changes are to be implemented, and that communication is essentially two-way traffic. Show that input from stakeholders really counts and helps to shape the programme. Ensure the right message from the right person reaches the right people, and that the information is clear and consistent. Give explicit consideration to any known discrepancies. Use language understood by everyone and keep it simple. Use as many different media as possible, making sure the message is repeated again and again. Listen and make sure stakeholders are heard. Communicate successes; nothing delivers more energy than jointly experienced successes.

6.6   How to get stakeholders involved

When the interests and influence of the different contacts are known, as well as their attitude to the programme, it is then possible to determine how the various stakeholders can best be involved in the programme. Basic possibilities are:
- Don't involve them
- Inform them
- Consult with them
- Involve them in the implementation
- Involve them in making decisions.

Not involving them, and therefore not even informing them, does not seem opportune in the context of a programme. Thought must be given to business competition and suchlike. Ignoring parties within a programme is not an option.

It is important to ascertain the desired shifts in relations between the various parties where a programme is concerned. A diagram indicating relations, as in figure 6.8, can easily be used for this purpose by also stating desired positions next to existing positions. Possible actions can also be determined based on this division of tasks.

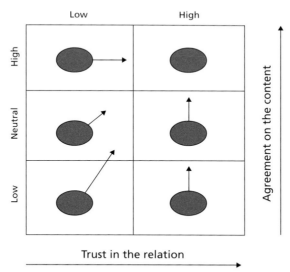

Fig. 6.8 Diagram indicating relations and stakeholder management tasks

Possible actions regarding various stakeholders:
- *Coalition partner:* it is particularly important to make concrete agreements on co-operation and the outcome to be delivered.
- *Ally:* these relations must be cherished. The more co-operation is possible, the better.
- *Opportunist:* it is not clear which standpoint to adopt when it comes down to it. Exploring the

69

possible benefits and clearly communicating these is very important.

- *Doubter:* the uncertainty often comes from the fact that they still do not know what the programme means to them. They can often generate more benefits and minimize costs if they are more informed and involved.
- *Adversary:* a business relationship can often be created by being clear about the goals and benefits to be realized, and how to approach them. It is important to separate the emotional and business aspects. It is often better to approach an adversary via an ally.
- *Opponent:* clarity is of great importance here. It is good to talk about the differences in understanding. It is also possible to talk about overlapping and conflicting interests.

It is essential in this context to establish how to process feedback from the stakeholders in the programme. This should not be on a pro forma, but on a tangible and open basis. Is there still a purpose to their contribution? At what point can the programme or parts of it still be adapted or set-up differently without this disturbing the process? What sort of input is required and how much margin is there? Within what margin can one still operate and who finally decides how to proceed?

Clear process agreements must be made on this in advance. Nothing is more frustrating to the process than the parties noticing later that the process is not going as they had envisaged.

Within programmes, the how and when regarding involvement of stakeholders must be ascertained at various admission levels. Is the Works Council involved in developing the vision, the Blueprint, the Programme Plan or just individual projects in the area of HRM? A complex system of informing, consulting, involving, deciding and giving feedback often applies to individual parties.

The input by these parties must often be included in the programme much earlier than generally thought. Time must be provided within the process to really give meaning to the involvement. An important point is that the parties' influence on the programme must also be seen. Communication and the approach to the programme are thus inseparable. Communication is often not a derivative of the programme approach; rather the programme approach is a derivative of communication.

6.7   Establishing the effectiveness of communication

Last but not least, as an element of Stakeholder Management Strategy, it must be established how the effectiveness of communication is tested during implementation. As with other plans, testing of communication activities and the Communication Plan must be based on reality and adjusted if necessary. This is too often done 'off the cuff', much too late or not at all.

How effectiveness of communication is tested, by whom, and when, must be established in advance. This must be tested against the objectives to be achieved with the communication. Information can be acquired by simple means such as surveys, interviews, lunches and 'management by walking around', or derived from the number of hits on a website, reactions from stakeholders, and such like.

6.8   Communication Plan

The Communication Plan is finally drawn up, based on the Stakeholder Management Strategy. The Communication Plan lays down what is communicated to whom, by whom, and via what medium. This plan must be set-up as early as possible in the definition phase, as communication in the definition phase is itself a factor. Based on the Communication Plan, communication agreements can then be optimized in this phase, such as those set at the end of the initial phase.

The aim of the Communication Plan is to ensure that:
• The main messages of the programme are spread
• It is clear to all stakeholders what the envisaged situation at the end of the programme is and what benefits are to be realized
• Commitment is created among colleagues and staff in the respective departments
• All people involved are informed as to the progress before, during and after implementation
• It is made clear that senior management is committed to the programme and is personally involved in realizing the benefits.

The Communication Plan must answer the following questions:
• What does one wish to achieve with each communication activity?
• What are the key messages in the communication?
• What are the target groups for the various communication activities?
• Who must communicate what information?
• When must the information be released?
• How much information will be released and in how much detail?
• How will the information be released and in which medium?
• How can parties provide feedback, how is this stimulated, how is the feedback processed and how is the outcome of this made clear?

6.9   Communication channels

It is important to use as many different communication channels as possible (see figure 6.9). Stakeholders feel best involved via various channels. As already mentioned, it essential to repeat the message again and again. Actively approach the stakeholders but give them the opportunity to take the information if it suits them (passive).

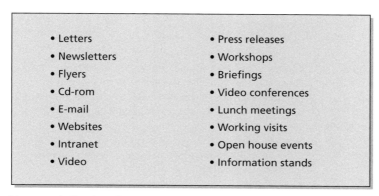

• Letters
• Newsletters
• Flyers
• Cd-rom
• E-mail
• Websites
• Intranet
• Video

• Press releases
• Workshops
• Briefings
• Video conferences
• Lunch meetings
• Working visits
• Open house events
• Information stands

Figure 6.9 Possible communication channels

The Programme Management Team must realize that, by good example, the management and the sponsors are themselves the most effective communication. Real commitment to the programme cannot be faked; lip service is insufficient. Daily activities by the managers must be governed by the changes to be implemented, and they must allow this to be seen through contacts with their staff.

Communication in a programme is not just another aspect of management or something with which all people are gifted. It is always a good idea to use professionals for this, even though management has the final decision in communication matters.

6.10 Responsibilities for stakeholder management

The Programme Manager is responsible for preparing the Stakeholder Management Strategy and the Communication Plan, and for implementing the Stakeholder Management Strategy into the programme. The Programme Management Team supports the Programme Manager in these tasks. The Programme Management Team will often include a communication expert, but the Programme Manager may also use a communication department within his own organization. The Senior Responsible Owner is finally responsible for the Stakeholder Management Strategy and must also approve the Communication Plan in this case.

The Business Change Managers are responsible for involving the various stakeholders in the changes within their own departments. The Senior Responsible Owner is responsible for committing the key figures.

The communication activities are carried out according to the Communication Plan. The Programme Office supports the people responsible and often arranges the information to be communicated. The Programme Manager monitors the implementation as far as progress, content and effectiveness are concerned. Furthermore, both the assessment of implementation and the effectiveness of the Stakeholder Management Strategy and communication are on the agenda in the gateway reviews. The Senior Responsible Owner is in charge of these reviews.

See table 6.1. for a summary of stakeholder management and communication responsibilities.

Role	Responsibilities
Senior Responsible Owner	Owner of Stakeholder Management Strategy
	Approving the Communication Plan
	Involving key personnel in the programme
	Being in charge of gateway reviews
Programme Manager	Drawing up and implementing Stakeholder Management Strategy
	Drawing up the Communication Plan
	Communication activities as laid down in the Communication Plan
	Monitoring stakeholder and communication activities
Business Change Manager	Involving stakeholders from their own business units
	Communication activities as laid down in the Communication Plan
Programme Office	Collecting and registering information for communication to the stakeholders
	Facilitating communication activities
Programme Management Team	Supports PrgM in preparing and implementing the Stakeholder Management Strategy and communication activities

Table 6.1 Responsibilities of stakeholder management and communication

7 Risk management and issue resolution

Every programme has opportunities, but also risks and issues. MSP offers an integral risk management and issue resolution approach. A risk involves the possibility that a fact or circumstance will transpire in the future and will have consequences later on in the process. An issue, or point of interest, is an event or situation that has occurred. It has an influence on the project or programme and requires the consideration of management in order to prevent or solve problems. A risk becomes an issue if it becomes a reality.

7.1 Introduction to risk management

One programme may have more risks or more serious risks than another, but there are always risks with any change. Dealing with these risks is therefore essential if the programme is to succeed. Risk management ensures that programme management has the correct information for decision-making and actions. Experience has shown that the phase where the greatest profit (most favourable cost/benefit ratio) is to be achieved is also the phase with the greatest risks. Risk management and benefits realization are therefore closely related to one another and have to be dealt with in the programme together. The goals of risk management are preventing unwanted situations and/or minimizing the effects when an undesired event occurs. Risk management enables programme management to reduce costs, reduce the energy invested in dealing with issues, and increase the programme's chances of success. Risk management involves maximizing the chance of the programme achieving the expected goals.

The Risk Management Strategy lays down how risks are identified, analysed and managed within a programme. This strategy is also the framework for the risk management approach of the underlying projects.

Risk management must be completely integrated into the programme and project management processes. It is better to follow a pragmatic approach and to communicate this clearly, rather than implementing a strict theory. It is a question of common sense in communication, and the use of a good method. It is also important to appoint risk owners for the individual risks. These are the people in the best position to keep an eye on the risk and to take countermeasures as necessary. It is also essential to have an open culture when it comes to risk management. Preventing guilt can be an enormous help in creating an open culture; there will be no openness if people start looking for scapegoats. Risk management must be directly linked to the benefits to be realized within the programme.

7.2 Risk Management Strategy

The risk management process is divided into various steps (see figure 7.1). Each step makes a contribution to managing the risks in a programme.
 The Risk Management Strategy is developed in the first step, and this involves how risks are dealt with in the programme. The Risk Management Strategy defines the necessary activities and

responsibilities for managing the programme risks. The strategy also provides the framework for managing the risks within the individual projects and states how agreement on the risks will take place between the projects and the programme. The foundations are also laid in this stage for the executive element of risk management at programme level. The Programme Manager is responsible for developing the Risk Management Strategy and for carrying out programme risk management on a daily basis.

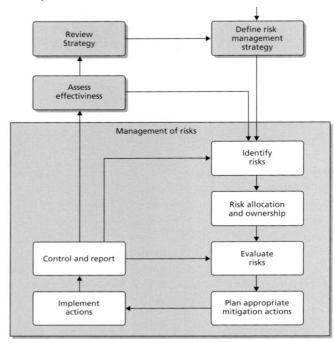

Fig. 7.1 Risk management process

The programme's Risk Management Strategy can be defined from that of the business organization. Lessons learned from previous programmes, and the personal experience of individual parties, can also be used. The Risk Management Strategy shows which approach is used for each of the subsequent steps.

7.3 Risk management

Risk management comprises two main elements: the risk analysis and risk management. The first element means the preparatory actions necessary for managing a risk. The second element deals with the risks identified.

Risk analysis within MSP includes risk identification, allocation, and evaluation and the selection of countermeasures.

7.3.1 Risk identification

Risk identification involves identifying risks for the programme. On identification, the risks will state what the threat to the programme is, and the risk category will also be set. The risks and risk categories are laid down in the Risk Register.

It is practically impossible to identify all risks to the programme. It is better to concentrate on the most important risks and thus aim at the twenty per cent of risks responsible for the eighty per cent of possible impact on the programme.

There are many ways to identify risks. A group of people can be formed to trace the risks in a brainstorming session, or by using checklists, a cause and effect diagram, sensitivity and scenario analyses and such like. A programme can be so large or complex that it may be wise to indicate risk areas and to have a meeting to discuss each area. There might, for example, be commercial, financial, legal, organizational and political risks.

Within MSP, distinction is made between risks on various levels, such as:
- *Strategic risks:*
  These are risks where there is the possibility that the benefits of a programme might not be realized. This could be the result of outside causes such as legislation or changing legal circumstances, the breach of a commitment on a strategic level within the business organization, or dependencies between programmes.
- *Programme risks:*
  These are risks arising from dependencies between the projects or apparent unjust assumptions upon which the Business Case is based. These also include risks arising from use, quality and capacity of the Programme Management Team itself.
- *Project risks:*
  These refer to events affecting efficiency in carrying out the project.
- *Operational risks:*
  These include risks connected with the setting-up and implementing of new business processes.

Identifying risks is an activity that remains ongoing throughout the entire programme. Risks change or cease, and new risks appear. It is important to remain alert for new risks that could prevent the programme from achieving its goals. Failing to recognize a risk is the greatest risk there is, as this means the risk cannot be managed. If the risk transpires, one can only act reactively and it is not possible to influence the extent of the risk's impact.

7.3.2 Risk allocation

Risk management is initially the Programme Manager's responsibility, but a risk owner must be allocated for each individual risk. The risk owner is the best person for 'keeping an eye' on the risk and taking countermeasures to manage the chance and/or the impact of the risk to the project or programme. The Programme Manager is often the risk owner, but Business Change Managers, Project Executives and Senior Responsible Owners can also be owners of specific risks. The Risk Register states who the owners of specific risks are.

7.3.3 Risk evaluation

For each identified risk, the risk evaluation determines how great the chance of occurrence is, and what the impact of the risk is on the project or programme if it becomes reality. With respect to the impact, consideration must be given to the costs and duration, as well as the possible benefits.

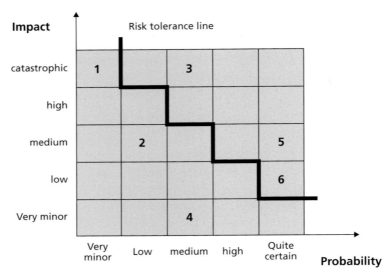

Fig. 7.2 Risk profile

A risk profile can be set-up based on chance multiplied by the impact (see figure 7.2). Tolerance levels for the risk must also be set-up. If the chance multiplied by the impact of a risk is higher than the risk tolerance, the risk owner must escalate this to the Programme Manager. The chance, the impact and the risk profile will be recorded in the Risk Register.

7.3.4 Selecting countermeasures
Countermeasures can be taken to reduce the chance and/or the impact of the risk to the project or programme. MSP refers to the four Ts:
- *Transfer:* the risk is transferred to another party, think of insurance, for example.
- *Tolerate:* the 'do nothing' option. The risk is acceptable.
- *Terminate:* the risk is removed, for example, by adjusting the programme or removing the element in which the risk might occur.
- *Treat:* the chances of occurring and/or the impact on occurrence is returned to an acceptable level.

An emergency plan can be set-up as well as the above measures, in case the risk materializes.

When accepting the risk, a decision is taken for the time being not to adopt any countermeasures, but it is necessary to keep a finger on the pulse as far as the risk is concerned. This is different from denying that there is a risk.

There are often several countermeasures available for one risk, in which case one must find out which ones are the most effective for the programme. A combination of countermeasures is often chosen. It is important to carry out a cost-benefit analysis when weighing up the various countermeasures. Risk measures can themselves introduce new risks or increase other existing risks. Careful consideration is necessary in order to arrive at an optimal mixture of measures. The approved countermeasures must be recorded in the Risk Register.

7.3.5 Implementing actions

The countermeasures are refined in more detail, after which another test is carried out to see if the countermeasures are still desired in light of the latest details. The plans will be included in the current Programme Plan, and then submitted again to the decision-making parties for final approval. Following approval, the funds required for implementing the plans will be made available and the measures implemented. Those people burdened by the risk, or who have to deal with the consequences of the countermeasures, will be informed. The Risk Register will be updated following implementation.

7.3.6 Monitoring and reporting

Based on reports, the Programme Manager can keep an eye on identified risks and provide the initiative for additional actions where necessary. The Risk Register will have to be amended if the status of a risk changes because the chance and/or the impact may have changed. The risk management process will have to be reviewed where necessary in order to cope adequately with the risk.

When communicating risks, it is important to match the message to the target group. Check to see how the information best supports the purpose of the communication. Matrix overviews and colour indications showing the status (traffic lights) can be used for this. The level of detail with which communications are carried out can also change. For the Sponsoring Group, only the most important risks on a strategic and programme level are shown.

7.4   Risk management assurance

Ensuring risk management includes setting-up, maintaining, assessing and evaluating risk management.

7.4.1 Testing effectiveness

The approach and set-up of risk management in the programme are checked regularly, at least at the end of each tranche. The purpose of this assessment is to check whether the measures taken are effective enough, whether the risks were identified in advance during the risk identification phase, and if they were taken seriously enough. Which issues could be forecast? This experience can be included in the 'Lesson Learned' Report.

7.4.2 Evaluating the Risk Management Strategy

It is not just important to check that risk management is efficiently carried out within the chosen strategy; it is also necessary to check whether the chosen strategy is the best one in the given circumstances. Are the chosen procedures and the allocated responsibilities still adequate or should these be adapted?

7.5   Introduction to issue resolution

A point of interest, or issue, is an actual problem, question, concern or request for change that influences the programme and requires consideration by Management in order to be solved. An issue can occur at any moment during a programme and will often require specific consideration by Management. These are mainly issues escalated from projects; they are issues that cannot be solved by the project or which are outside its tolerance boundaries.

Issue resolution is the process that ensures that issues are managed. The aim of issue resolution is to efficiently prevent an issue getting in the way of a programme successfully realizing its goals. The process includes collecting, registering and analysing issues, decision-making, and initiating and monitoring the agreed actions.

Figure 7.3 shows the issue resolution process. This proceeds from collecting and registering the issues through to their being dealt with. All programme issues must be entered into a register. The Programme Manager is responsible for managing the programme issues.

Issue resolution also ensures that programme management has the correct information in order to arrive at a decision regarding programme issues.

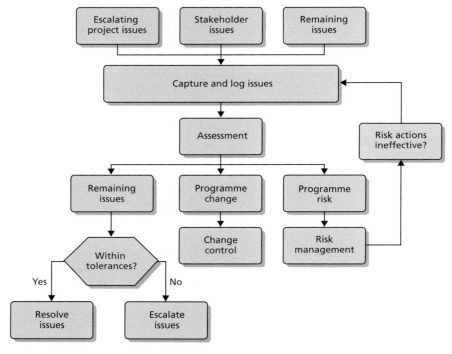

Figure 7.3 Issue resolution process (© Crown copyright 2003 reproduced under licence from HMSO)

7.6 Issue resolution strategy

Issue Resolution Strategy specifies how issues are managed. The strategy provides answers to how the issue resolution process (shown in figure 7.3) takes shape. It also states the difference and the relationship between the issue resolution process within projects and the issue resolution process within a programme. The Stakeholder and Risk Management Strategy provides input in establishing the Issue Resolution Strategy. Experience with earlier programmes also provides input for determining the correct strategy.

The Issue Resolution Strategy defines how the necessary issue evaluation can be acquired, who is responsible for solving issues and how owners are allocated to issues.

It is important to prioritize because several issues can arise in a programme. Criteria are also defined in the Issue Resolution Strategy, based on which priorities can be set within the programme.

7.7   Issue resolution

7.7.1 Issue analysis

Issues can arise from several sources, which can be diverse within large and complex programmes. Examples of sources are:
• An earlier identified risk occurring. The required measure for managing the risk is defined as an issue
• Benefits management and transition activities
• Process monitoring, budget monitoring and resource management
• Dependencies and relations between projects, and between benefits and projects
• Operational processes
• Escalated projects or issues exceeding projects
• Stakeholders, business organization, Programme Management Team and third parties
• Other projects, programmes and initiatives within the organization
• External and internal environment within the organization.

Every issue that occurs must be recorded in the Issue Log and then analysed. The Programme Manager is responsible for analysing the issues. It must be established what kind of issue it is, what priority applies and what follow-up action is required.

The issues can be distinguished into two types:
• A necessary change to the programme
• A problem, question or event with a consequence for the entire programme or part of it.

Requests for change are dealt with by Change Control. This is a part of con-figuration management but comes under issue resolution as regards management of programme documents.

Issues can also refer to possible future events, in which case they are actually risks and should be handled as such. They must be entered in the Risk Register and then come under the risk management process.

The other issues are prioritized and consideration is given to how far the issues can be solved within the existing parameters of the Programme Manager's authority. He will take action for the issues within his remit, record the results in the Issue Log, and report these back to the person who reported the issue. He will escalate issues outside his authority to the person responsible, record this, and also report this to the person who reported the issue. Within the programme, the Programme Manager reports issues exceeding his authority to the Senior Responsible Owner.

7.7.2 Programme issues

Some issues can affect further elements of the programme or even other programmes. Such issues must be managed with the programme's issue resolution process. These issues have a high priority in connection with the major impact of possible corrective measures on the programme and the business organization.

Issues that have an impact on other programmes can, for example, be due to capacity problems in the deployment of staff and resources, relations with stakeholders, and questions regarding costs and financing of the programmes.

Such issues must be escalated to senior management within the organization. It is important that the members of the Programme Management Team maintain effective communication with senior management, particularly in periods during which many such issues occur that are outside the scope of the programmes.

7.7.3 Change Control

Changes within a programme must be monitored scrupulously. A change at the start of a programme can have an enormous impact on the viability of the programme, and may never be implemented without authorization. Change Control within the programme involves managing the changes to the key documents, which together form the Programme Definition and the underlying plans.

The following are possible procedures for Change Control:
- Recording requests for change in the Issue Log, setting the first priority, reacting to misunderstandings and informing the applicant as to the registration
- Analysing the consequences of the change to various programme documents, such as the Business Case, the Programme Plan and the Blueprint. Particular attention should be paid to the consequences regarding the risks and the benefits to be achieved
- Re-evaluating the priority of the request for change
- Preparing the request for change (with substantiated advice) for decision-making
- Updating the Issue Log following the decision and giving feedback on the decision to the applicant
- Implementing agreed changes, monitoring the actions and outcome, and recording the final result in the Issue Log.

7.7.4 Relationship between project and programme

All project risks and issues should be visible for the programme. The individual Project Teams do not always have sufficient insight into which risks and issues could have an impact on other projects within the programme, or on the programme as a whole. The final responsibility for all issues within the programme is with programme management level, particularly with the Programme Manager.

In practice, it is wise to manage the risks and issues where the parties have the best view of them, where they experience the most 'nuisance' from them, and can exert the most influence on handling them. This could be at the individual project level.

Each Project Team within the programme has responsibility for the risk and issue resolution process within its own projects. For managing the programme, it is advisable to standardize these processes across the programme's entire portfolio.

Programme management sets the tolerance levels for the individual projects, as well as the escalation levels for the issues. It is important to find a balance between managing issues on the programme level and the possible administrative and bureaucratic rigmarole that can be involved. The Programme Office must be given a central role in the risks and issue resolution process of both the programme and the projects.

The Programme Office can simply streamline the various processes and maintain effective two-way communication between the programme and the various projects.

Managing issues is a continuous process and must be carried out throughout the entire programme. Much implementation work, such as updating information and the programme's Issue Log, can be carried out by the Programme Office. Automated systems can help in handling and processing issues, and collecting information can be made easier by removing any barriers to issues.

7.8   Issue resolution assurance

Assurance of issue resolution involves setting-up, maintaining, assessing and evaluating issue resolution.

As with risk management assurance, when providing assurance for issue resolution, checks must be made as to whether the issue resolution is well carried out within the chosen strategy, and whether this is the best strategy in the given circumstances. The approach to issue resolution must be checked regularly, at least at the end of each tranche.

7.9   Responsibilities

The Senior Responsible Owner is finally responsible for risk and issue resolution of the programme. The Programme Manager is responsible for the daily carrying out of risk and issue resolution. The Business Change Managers must ensure that risks and issues regarding their own benefits are well managed. The Programme Office is responsible for following up the risk and issue resolution procedures within the programme. The Programme Office also maintains the respective Issue Logs. Risk owners should keep a watchful eye on risks allocated to them. The Programme Management gives the framework for the risk and issues management within the underlying projects.

See table 7.1 for an overview of the responsibilities of risk- and issue resolution.

Role	Responsibilities
Senior Responsible Officer	Ensuring that risk and issue resolution are adequately implemented
	Ensuring that the critical risks and issues are suitably dealt with
Programme Manager	Preparing and implementing the risk and Issue Resolution Strategy
Business Change Manager	Ensuring that all risks and issues regarding the realization of benefits remain within tolerance levels
Programme Office	Collecting, registering and analysing the risks and issues
	Monitoring the agreed measures and ensuring that actions are carried out on time
Risk owner	Managing specific risks
Relevant authority	Solving specific issues

Table 7.1 Responsibilities in risk and issue resolution

8 Programme planning and management

8.1 Introduction

Programme planning- and management is not just a list of the various project plans and management agreements. The Programme Plan is a key document in the programme; it is the result of a vision, the Blueprint to be realized, as well as the benefits and uncertainties in adjusting the programme to the business goals (see figure 8.1). The Programme Plan is therefore the framework for the individual project plans, and not the other way around. The Programme Plan also includes the main parts of the transition plans for the various changes to be implemented, thus ensuring a direct relationship with the Benefits Realization Plan.

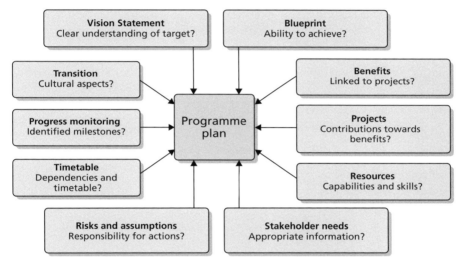

Fig. 8.1 Input for the Programme Plan (© Crown copyright 2003 reproduced under licence from HMSO)

Vision Statement

The programme's Vision Statement describes the end goal that the organization wishes to achieve with the programme. It provides a description of the new capabilities that the organization requires for this in terms of new services, better performance, innovation and possibly an improved attitude towards clients and users.

Blueprint

The Blueprint describes the new organization that has been realized at the end of the programme. This description includes the organizational adjustments in tasks, responsibility and authority and with respect to skills, attitude and behaviour. The Blueprint also includes adjustments in the processes to be carried out, the infrastructure, and the provision of information required in order to substantiate the new resources as described in the Vision Statement.

Benefits

Realizing the benefits anticipated with the achievement of the programme's end goal is crucial for the programme's success. The benefits are established in benefits profiles and must be included in the Benefits Realization Plan according to the diagram. The Benefits Realization Plan and the Programme Plan must be closely adjusted to one another.

Projects

The projects and activities as described in the Project Portfolio will produce the future end situation as described in the Blueprint as well as the resources necessary to realize the benefits and the programme's end goal.

Use of staff and resources

The Programme Plan provides input for defining the necessary staff and resources to realize the programme. This involves the necessary effort for the projects and for the normal business activities envisaged. When deploying staff, their skills are at least as important as the required resources.

Stakeholders

The Programme Plan is a key document in the Programme and includes essential information important for many parties. On the other hand, information from the various parties involved in the programme will influence the Programme Plan and help to shape it.

Risks

No programmes exist without uncertainties; these uncertainties are anticipated by taking management measures. A margin is also introduced into the programme in order to cope with new situations.

Timing

The reason for starting a programme often delivers specific milestones that are the precondition for the programme. Certain deadlines that must be met depend on other programmes and initiatives.

Progress monitoring

It is essential for each plan that the progress of activities provided for in the plan is monitored and updated. This also applies to the Programme Plan. The plan establishes how this is to be monitored and updated, and it will be ascertained at which points the progress of the entire programme is to be evaluated. The Programme Plan must be updated throughout the entire programme.

Transition

Transition management includes the co-ordinated organization, control and implementation of a change in order to realize one or more pre-defined objectives. It is essential to leave behind the old way of working, and a new way of working will be accepted and transformed as the new 'business as usual'. All activities necessary for such transition must be meticulously planned. The transition is necessary in order to realize the final benefits on completion of the project results and is therefore essential in achieving the objectives.

Transition management is the link between realizing projects and realizing benefits. Cultural aspects also play a crucial role in implementing changes.

The individual transition plans needed to incorporate the results achieved through the plans and activities in the organizations involved. They are prepared by the Programme Manager, together with the respective Business Change Manager. These individual plans provide input for the transition plans in broad terms, as included in the Programme Plan.

8.2 Programme Planning

Programme Planning is a continuous process initiated in the Programme Definition phase and it lasts for the entire programme. The Programme Plan includes the projects to be implemented, the mutual dependences, the uncertainties , how these uncertainties are and will be anticipated, the transition plan and how and by whom the plans are to be monitored and updated.

The Programme Manager also prepares the transition plan but in close cooperation with the Business Change Managers. The transition plan specifies when the project results will be delivered to the respective business units and what transition activities are envisaged for implementing the new resources and imbedding the changes into the new organization. The transition plan is based on the individual transition plans of the Business Change Managers.

Programme Planning demands continuous harmonization between projects and also between projects/transitions and the realization of benefits. Account must also be taken of external projects, programmes and initiatives. The focus on Programme Planning is on optimizing this harmonization in and outside the programme.

The most important steps in Programme Planning are:
- Setting-up the Project Portfolio with the projects and activities needed to realize the new resources
- Determining the project planning that fits in with the Benefits Realization Plan
- Continuous harmonization between refined individual project plans on the one hand and the projects and benefits to be realized on the other
- Anticipating incidents whereby adjustments to the Programme Plan are required
- Continuously monitoring progress of the activities and projects with respect to the Programme Plan and updating the plan, including the anticipation of issues arising from uncertainties and which might affect the programme's progress.

8.3 Project Portfolio

The first thing to do when preparing a Programme Plan is to set-up the Project Portfolio, which includes all projects and associated activities necessary to deliver the defined outcomes according to the Blueprint. For each project, a summary is included of the end result, as well as the timing, the necessary deployment of staff and resources, and the dependencies with other projects and initiatives.

This also shows which benefits will be made possible by the individual projects, either individually or in combination with other projects (see figure 8.2).

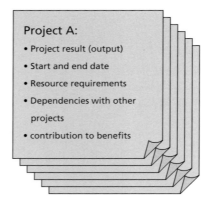

Project A:

• Project result (output)

• Start and end date

• Resource requirements

• Dependencies with other

  projects

• contribution to benefits

Fig. 8.2 Project Portfolio

The Project Portfolio is derived from the Blueprint and the benefits profiles. The Programme Manager prepares the Project Portfolio.

8.4   Project dependency network

Based on the Project Portfolio, a project dependency network will be set-up to show the time dependencies between the individual projects (see figure 8.3). The project dependency network indicates for each project the input needed for starting the project and the output (project result) delivered by the project.

Each project is seen as a black box and is not divided into various activities. It can, however, be a good idea to divide projects that generate partial benefits into subprojects. The project dependency network gives the Programme Manager insight into dependencies between projects and the impact caused by delays.

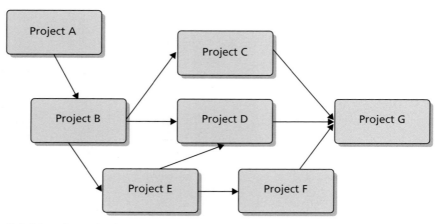

Fig. 8.3 Project dependency network

8.5   Programmes tranches

Programme tranches can be based on the Project Portfolio and the project dependency network. A programme tranche is a connected group of projects, which together enables a new level of performance within the programme (see figure 8.4). Programme tranches can be linked to a location or based on a certain infrastructure, a specific business unit or service. Programme tranches are often given a name so that people who work on them identify with them.

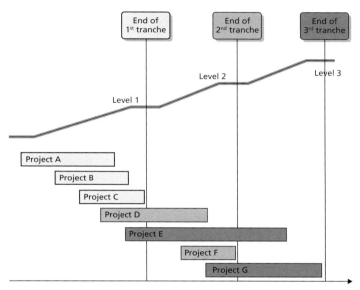

Figure 8.4 Programme tranches and transition between levels (© Crown copyright 2003 reproduced under licence from HMSO)

A programme tranche ends as soon as the last project within the tranche has been delivered. Programme tranches might overlap. The final points of the programme tranches whereby a new performance level is made possible within the organization are, by definition, far apart. The period between reaching one level is often given the name of the last tranche, and with long-running programmes, the transition from one level to the next is often linked to the operational planning cycle.

On reaching each new level, the programme is normally reviewed as regards the operation and the outcome achieved. The relevant programme documents are then updated, particularly the Benefits Realization Plan and the Programme Plan. Checks will also be carried out at the point of transition from one level to the next to see whether the additional benefits to be generated based on the next performance level still weigh up against the enablers, or whether resources and enablers would be better spent on other business goals. It is important to see whether any subsequent phase should still be carried out within the context of the programme or be postponed with other tasks in the operational areas. If it is decided not to continue the programme, it must be formally closed and the remaining tasks transferred to the individual business units.

8.6   Use of staff and resources

A strategy for the use of staff and resources must be established to cover: what resources are required, how to ensure that these resources will be available on time, how the resources will be managed and how to ensure that staff and resources will be used as efficiently and effectively as possible?

In order to establish the strategy, the programme projects and activities will have to be estimated, the programme budget will have to be set and liquidity planning arranged. Based on this, the necessary financing can be established and the best way to finance the programme can be decided. This is normally determined together with the client organization's finance department. The accountants and procurement procedures must finally be established and agreements made as to the financial reports that need to be prepared.

The work by one's own staff and that of suppliers must be determined for implementing various projects and business activities, not just regarding capacity but also regarding skills required. It is also necessary to determine how resources will be deployed after any changes have been implemented. The impact on staff deployment can be enormous and must take account of social and career planning aspects. The support required from the HRM Department must also be established, both for the required staff deployment or reduction and for supervising the required transition.

The use and application of resources must also be determined regarding buildings, machines and ICT infrastructure, and supporting services. This requires not just determining the application of the resources for realizing the programme, but also the altered application of resources resulting from the changes implemented.

Finally, it must be determined how to jointly apply staff and resources as effectively and efficiently as possible in various locations or for various purposes such as:
• Persons capable of working for various projects
• Joint use of facilities
• Information that can be used by various units
• Supporting services.

The strategy for the deployment of staff and resources must be developed in parallel with the Programme Plan. The Programme Manager is responsible for developing this strategy.

8.7   Managing a programme

Where a project is aimed at delivering a project result, a programme must be aimed at delivering various capabilities as well as realizing the benefits defined. Managing a programme therefore differs considerably from managing a project.

Managing a programme need not be aimed at individual activities within a project, but should concentrate on managing projects globally. It is important that before the project, relevant programme information is provided to the project and that correct and sufficient information from the project is supplied to the programme.

The greatest challenge in the interaction between the programme and the projects is to ensure that the Project Management Team assumes its responsibilities regarding project management, but also that the projects are controlled by the programme without the Programme Manager taking over control of all the projects. This would mean the Programme Manager gaining too much focus on the implementation of projects and paying too little attention to the progress made in realizing the benefits. With such a level of control, the group of parties involved in the various projects, and thus also with the programme, is limited, which is normally not conducive to commitment within the organization.

If the Programme Manager co-ordinates the projects remotely, it is important to ensure that available information can be used directly within the programme. This is possible by a one-on-one use of the information from the project proposal, the project initiation document, the reports on the main issues, the end-stage reports and the end-project reports. It is also important to ensure that the report templates for all projects within the programme are the same.

The most important aspects to be harmonized between the programme and the individual projects are:
• Relevant changes in the programme, for example, amendments to the Vision Statement, the Blueprint or the Business Case
• Responsibilities and the ownership of risks and actions following issues at programme level with an influence on the project level
• Project tolerance levels regarding costs, time, scope, quality, risks and the benefits to be realized
• Allocating staff and resources to projects
• Milestones and go/no go points for the project.

8.8   Progress review and performance measurement

It is important for the progress evaluation that both the processes and the activities carried out are assessed. The Programme Plan must continuously show the status of the programme, and it is important to give consideration to the most critical projects.

It is also important to define all project results according to the acronym SMART. The progress of the projects can be monitored in various ways. The normal way is to express the progress in a prepared percentage and to set this against incurred expenses and time. A more modern method is the Earned Value Analysis, whereby it is also possible, based on planned and realized progress, to make an estimation of total expenses and the expected completion date.

When measuring performance, it is important to agree clearly and in advance with the Business Change Manger the critical performance indicators, the associated measuring method, and the original baseline measurement. The changed circumstances will always remain, which place earlier agreements under pressure. It can be determined in advance to what extent external factors play a role in the performance to be delivered, and to what extent the performance depends on this. A known performance measurement is the INK model. Chapter 20 includes a short summary of various performance methods.

It is important with both the progress monitoring and performance measuring to carry out an assessment of time and costs to be spent on these, and the total benefits or costs managed. There is no point spending thousands of euros/dollars in monitoring the results if the overall benefits only amount to a few hundred euros/dollars.

8.9 Programme Plan

The Programme Plan is not a single authorized project plan, but gives a total overview of the entire programme (see figure 8.5). The Programme Plan must continuously show the latest situation of events regarding the entire programme.

```
Programme Plan

• Project Portfolio

• Project dependency network

• Risks and assumptions

• Relative sequence of projects, tranches and milestone
  review points

• Communication activities, risk mitigation activities
  and review work at programme level

• Transition plan to embed the new capabilities

• Monitoring and control activities
```

Fig. 8.5 Programme Plan

When setting-up the Programme Plan, it is important to develop a sense of the level of detail necessary to monitor and manage the programme. Which techniques can best be used for monitoring progress and measuring performance achieved? What is the best way to present the status and progress of the programme to the respective stakeholders? Which information should be distributed from the Programme Plan, to whom, when and how? The latter is an element of the planned communication activities.

8.10 Responsibilities

The Programme Manager is responsible for preparing and implementing the Programme Plan and the Resource Management Strategy. The Business Change Managers are responsible for managing the transition.

They must also ensure that the Project Portfolio and project planning facilitate and optimise the realization of benefits planned. The Programme Office supports the Programme Manager in developing and implementing planning and management activities, and it is responsible for collecting, registering and distributing information necessary for managing the programme.

See table 8.1 for an overview of the responsibilities for programme planning and management.

Role	Responsibilities
Senior Responsible Owner	Approving the Programme Plan
	Controlling the monitoring of progress and performance measurements
	Heading tranche reviews
Programme Manager	Drafting and carrying out of:
	• Programme Plan
	• Resource Management Strategy
	• Monitoring and controlling
Business Change Managers	Transition management
	Helping to draft the Project Portfolio and project planning in order to ensure the projects and the transition fit in with the planned realization of the benefits
Programme Office	Supporting the Programme Manager in collecting and distributing data
	Document management

Table 8.1 Responsibilities in programme planning and management

9   Business Case management

9.1   Introduction

The Business Case describes the corporate justification for a programme. It includes information on the goals to be realized and the associated benefits, costs, time and risks involved in implementing the programme.

The Business Case indicates how viable the programme is, to what extent the programme fits in with the business goals and strategies, how realistic the end goal is and whether the programme is desired in the light of other goals and initiatives within the organization. The Business Case indicates the actual value of the programme for the various parties involved with it.

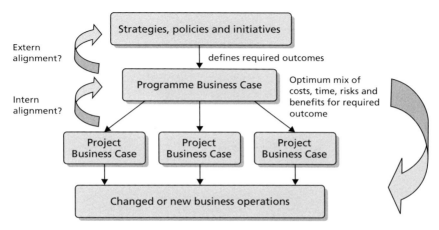

Fig. 9.1 Programme- and project Business Cases (© Crown copyright 2003 reproduced under licence from HMSO)

Within the framework of the programme, there are separate Business Cases for individual projects or programme tranches. Results produced with the help of projects can be realized in several ways, each producing different benefits. Each project therefore needs its own Business Case, as it must be established separately for each specific project if there is sufficient justification to implement it (see figure 9.1).

The programme's Business Case is the framework within which the scope and the goals of the project are determined and in which the project's Business Case must fit. The various project Business Cases together form the programme Business Case. Setting-up these Business Cases, which are interconnected, is thus a repetitive process. The programme Business Case must be regularly updated during the programme.

9.2   Developing the Business Case

The Business Case for the programme is evaluated at each point, before work on the programme is commenced.

It is possible that business goals have been set and business strategies developed at an early stage, and each one of these goals and strategies will have its own Business Case.

Before a programme can be started, various alternatives are often developed on the highest strategic level. Based on these senior management will decide the final direction in which the organization will develop. These alternatives are often evaluated in the form of a feasibility study or a 'master plan study'. The main aspects of a Business Case will be decided for each alternative within such a study. A decision for further development will be made based on the business strategies, and the initiative taken to commence the chosen programme.

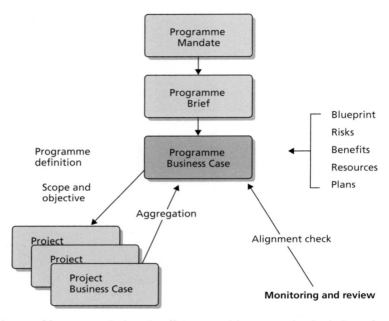

Fig. 9.2 Development of the programme Business Case (© Crown copyright 2003 reproduced under licence from HMSO)

The Programme Mandate is the initiative of the business management for starting the programme. The initiative is preferably laid down in a document, in which the programme is defined in basic terms and positioned within the framework of the business mission, objectives, strategies and other initiatives. The Programme Mandate leads to the initiation of the 'Identifying a programme' process.

In the 'Identifying a programme' process, the Programme Brief is developed, based on the Programme Mandate, by the future Senior Responsible Owner. The Programme Brief describes the main points of the programme. It contains the first step regarding objectives, desired benefits, risks, issues, costs and timing of the programme. The Programme Brief is the basis on which the Sponsoring Group approves the programme and issues authorization for starting the Programme Definition phase. It is also the basis for the Programme Definition and thus also for the Business Case (see figure 9.2).

The Business Case for the programme is developed as a separate document in the Programme Definition phase. However, much of the information on which the Business Case is based is to be found in previous documents.

9.3   What the Business Case involves

The Business Case is developed in direct connection with the Blueprint during the Programme Definition phase. The Blueprint describes the capabilities of the future organization; it initially shows the basis for the changes to be implemented, the end goal to be realized, the benefits to be achieved and the associated risks. The Blueprint also indicates the basis for the projects and activities necessary for realizing the future situation, and the associated costs and risks.

Risks

The programme involves risks both in realizing the capabilities and reaping the expected benefits. Risks are an essential factor in evaluating the corporate justification for the programme, and are therefore an essential factor in the Business Case.

Costs and benefits

The direct costs and expected benefits of a new development are extremely important to the Business Case. It is important to realize that income and expenses over the various years cannot simply be added together; income over ten years compared with current expenses have entirely different economic and emotional values.

The difference in economic value arises as future amounts can be generated through much smaller amounts by simply depositing the money in the bank or borrowing from the bank. For an accurate comparison of income and expenditure over various years, it is normal procedure to re-convert all amounts to today's date, based on the net present value method. The difference in emotional value arises from the fact that future money is more uncertain and cannot be used as freely; the flexibility of use and the possibility of enterprise are lower.

It is therefore important to spread expected income and expenditure over time, but beware of apparent accuracy. Many assumptions must be made with such calculations, so there is no point in placing two figures after the decimal point.

Time

Time is another important aspect in reviewing the Business Case. It is not only a factor in calculating the net present value, but also a simple shift in time on capabilities to be delivered might influence the Business Case negatively.
 For the development of a new consumer article, the delay in introduction might have a negative effect on six aspects:
• Delay in introducing leads to additional development costs
• Income will be less due to the delay, and the money will be worth less due to the effect of time
• The economic life will be less due to the delay. New products in a few years will mean the end of the application of the products to be developed. This end date does not normally move at the same pace, meaning the repayment period becomes shorter
• Other suppliers will be on the market sooner and thus gain a larger share of the market

- The delay will mean that the high sales prices incurred due to introducing new products on the market will benefit the competitors and bypass the organization
- The initial production expenses will be relatively higher due to the shorter economic life span, which could have dramatic consequences. The time factor can also have a great impact on the Business Case of developments within other organizations and even government bodies.

Programme goals

Last but not least, fitting in with the business goals is the most important aspect on which the Business Case is evaluated. Is the programme consistent with the business goals and other initiatives of the organization? Is there sufficient need for implementing the programme and do all parties involved realize this? Does the entire organization show the same level of ambition for the programme?

If the answer is not wholeheartedly "yes" here, then there is not a perfect fit between business goals and strategies, and this will in all probability be the greatest resistance against implementing the programme. If really large investments are required for the programme, and if staff and other stakeholders start to notice what the programme means for them, some strong arguments will be needed to justify it.

9.4   Review of Business Case

The programme's Business Case must be regularly updated throughout the entire programme. This is necessary to show the most up-to-date status of the programme and as a permanent benchmark for the programme's viability for the business organization.

The Business Case is one of the key documents that must be evaluated and approved before the Sponsoring Group can approve the entire programme at the end of the Programme Definition phase, and then issue authority to implement the programme. The Business Case must be updated at least at the end of each tranche and be value-tested during the programme evaluations. The programme's Business Case will have to be updated and evaluated in the meantime, as soon as there is a risk of costs, benefits, time or risks exceeding accepted tolerance levels.

Finally, the Business Case must be updated when closing the programme and in the case of various post-programme evaluations.

9.5   Managing the Business Case

The Business Case is not, in principle, a document with a high level of detail. The uncertainties regarding the environment, the business goals, the benefits to be realized and the costs and time for realizing the necessary capabilities are considerable. Resistance in organizations, market opportunities and successes are difficult issues for which there are no simple formulae.

The programme should, however, be taken into consideration. A best estimation is better than no estimation; the estimations must not assume the character of calculations, as with concrete projects or subsequent accounting calculations. The level of calculation will be similar to that of the business plans and strategies. The Business Case calculations, and those for the business plans for the organization, will be of the same magnitude and level of accuracy.

Calculations are necessary for reaching decisions; decisions are not made with good intentions alone. The necessity needs to be visible. There may be other projects and programmes that promise the earth, but concrete income today is better than nice words for the future.

Of course, the computer models used to calculate the Business Case will deliver exact figures, but this is just apparent accuracy. Small changes in input to these models often entail large changes in output. It is advisable to consider other scenarios, as this will often give a much better picture of the viability of the Business Case than a business calculation, however accurate it appears.

Costs and benefits in the course of the programme can be estimated more accurately. Ensure that the possibility of calculating something accurately is not simply the reason for so doing; accurate calculations should only be carried out if this is worthwhile.

9.6   Responsibilities

The Programme Manager is responsible for preparing and updating the Business Case and for managing expenditure versus the investment plan. The Business Change Managers identify and quantify the benefits and determine the best measuring means. They also ensure that the change is implemented and the benefits realized. The Programme Office collects and maintains the necessary information. The Senior Responsible Owner is finally responsible for realizing the end goal of the programme and ensures that the programme still fits in with the business strategy.

See table 9.1 for an overview of responsibilities in managing the Business Case.

Role	Responsibilities
Senior Responsible Owner	Final responsibility for delivering the end goal programme and is owner of the BC
	Ensuring the BC is monitored, evaluated and updated
	Ensuring that progress is consistent with starting points of the BC
Programme Manager	Preparing and updating the BC
	Managing expenditure versus investment plan
Business Change Managers	Identifying and defining the benefits
	Establishing the measuring method and implementing the baseline measurement
	Implementing the change and realizing the benefits
Programme Office	Collecting and maintaining information in connection with the Business Case
Programme Management Team	Specific expertise

Table 9.1 Responsibilities for managing the Business Case

10 Quality management

10.1 Introduction

The success of a change depends, among other things, on the degree with which the capabilities realized fit in with the needs and expectations of the users. A change will only be successful if the stakeholders are satisfied with the quality delivered, and if the products supplied efficiently and effectively support the new method of working. Quality is therefore an important condition for successfully implementing changes.

Quality is the degree to which product characteristics are in a position to satisfy an entire range of explicit and implicit needs. Quality management is the process for ensuring that clients' expectations are met, and it deals with activities, executive staff and products. It is essential that quality assessment criteria are prepared for all quality aspects in advance.

These criteria are the basis for all agreements on the quality of goods to be delivered and for how these are drawn up. The criteria help form a joint and controllable vision for what must be delivered and how. They are quality criteria: with what must the goods supplied comply? They are also acceptance criteria: under which conditions are the goods supplied acceptable? Here, it is a good idea to look for criteria that are requirements and must be satisfied, and for those criteria that are less 'hard'. A distinction is often made between: what is necessary (demand), what is useful (desire) and what would be nice (a dream)? References to precious metals are also made: "Shall we go for bronze" (only what is necessary), "silver" (what is necessary and useful) or "gold" (everything that is necessary, useful and pleasant)? Of course, these decisions are not isolated, as "gold" also has a golden price tag. The costs must be weighed up against the benefits.

With programme management, quality agreements must be made regarding the leadership and management of the programme, the management processes, products to be delivered and measurement, control and assessment activities.

Quality management is a continuous process that must be enshrined in daily activities within the process.

10.2 Quality Management Strategy

Quality management includes:
- *The quality system:* the series of procedures and instructions for carrying out quality assurance, including tasks, responsibilities and authorities of necessary people
- *The quality assurance:* including setting-up, maintaining, controlling and implementing evaluation of the effectiveness of the quality system
- *The planning of all quality activities:* setting-up the quality criteria, applying the quality system, the quality assurance, carrying out quality control and providing necessary staff and resources.
- *Quality management:* quality controls to verify whether all products to be delivered satisfy the necessary specifications.

The Quality Management Strategy defines the approach to quality management within the programme. The Quality Management Strategy also lays down the framework for managing the quality of underlying projects and activities within the programme.

The Quality Management Strategy describes:
- The aspects of the programme that are to be managed via the quality system, and the quality criteria applicable
- Who will carry out the quality assurance, review, and management activities
- The planning of the quality activities to be carried out, and whether these activities are periodic, event or risk driven
- Which corrective measures will be taken, depending on the result of the evaluations
- Configuration Management and Change Control procedures
- Who is responsible for quality management
- The information necessary to adequately carry out quality management
- The supporting instruments for the various quality management activities, such as software for Configuration Management and Change Control activities
- Staff and resources necessary for implementing quality management.

The Programme Manager is responsible for preparing the strategy and must ensure that work is carried out according to the agreed strategy. The Senior Responsible Owner is ultimately responsible for the choice of strategy and for the integral quality of the programme.

10.3 Configuration management

Configuration Management is a part of quality management; it involves management of all 'items' in a programme organization. This involves all products, which have been or are being realized by the programme organization, the total of which is referred to as the 'configuration'. The individual items are referred to as configuration items (CIs). The standardization for Configuration Management is laid down in ISO Directive 10007. For the programme, the configuration items must also be established and managed using Configuration Management. Only by managing these items well can organizations work effectively and efficiently. The level to which the various CIs must be laid down and managed within the programme is stipulated in the programme's configuration management plan.

Configuration Management demands adequate Change Control. The link between them is that Configuration Management keeps the status information updated, while Change Control is responsible for the controlled implementation of changes. Change Control involves logging and prioritizing changes, carrying out impac-t analyses, arranging decision-making and implementing, controlling and communicating changes. Configuration Management involves planning, identifying, controlling, reporting and verifying the configuration of the configuration items (see figure 10.1). Change Control of configuration items is part of Configuration Management.

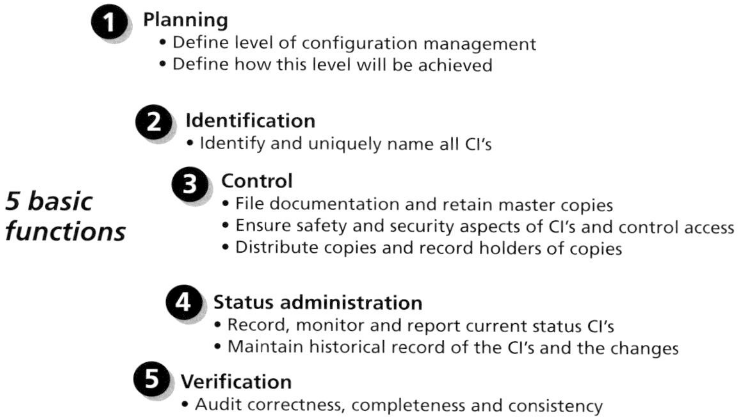

1 **Planning**
 • Define level of configuration management
 • Define how this level will be achieved

2 **Identification**
 • Identify and uniquely name all CI's

5 basic functions

3 **Control**
 • File documentation and retain master copies
 • Ensure safety and security aspects of CI's and control access
 • Distribute copies and record holders of copies

4 **Status administration**
 • Record, monitor and report current status CI's
 • Maintain historical record of the CI's and the changes

5 **Verification**
 • Audit correctness, completeness and consistency

Fig. 10.1 Configuration management activities

10.3.1 Configuration items

A configuration item is any product or item whose status requires management. A distinction can be made between programme CIs, external and internal CIs. Programme CIs include documents drawn up within the programme in the context of programme management, such as the Vision Statement, the Blueprint, the Business Case, the Programme Plan and the Benefits Realization Plan. External CIs are configuration -items from outside the programme, which still need to be managed. Examples are the organization strategy or policy documents serving as main points for the programme. Amendments to these documents can have a considerable effect on the programme. The inter-nal CIs are the results delivered by the underlying projects and activities.

This division can help to indicate which configuration items require managing via the programme Configuration Management. There is no point just including everything within the programme in the Configuration Management database (database of all CIs). Each item must be managed, so it is important to decide which items will and will not be included and the level of detail with which each item is to be described. The more detail applied, the more energy will be invested in the management. Configuration Management also requires the costs and benefits to be weighed up. But whatever decision is made, ensure that the CIs included are unique and recorded in a clear manner.

The configuration database must include the CI status, and here at least the statuses of 'draft', 'approved' and 'expired' must be distinguished. Other statuses may be included, such as 'for review', etc. The configuration database must also include the various stages in developing the CI, how these stages are assessed for approval and who grants this.

10.3.2 Configuration baselines

A baseline is a (connected) series of approved configuration items. A programme baseline can only be amended on instructions from the Senior Responsible Owner, and it is blocked until its status is formally changed. Baselines are pretty much the milestones of a programme. Expired baselines must be maintained for the archive; this makes it possible to establish the historical stages of the CIs. Status reports will make it possible to rely on previous versions of configuration items, should this be necessary. The baselines form a reference framework to which progress can be related and consistency evaluated. The baselines from the highest level can also be retraced to the criteria serving as the starting point.

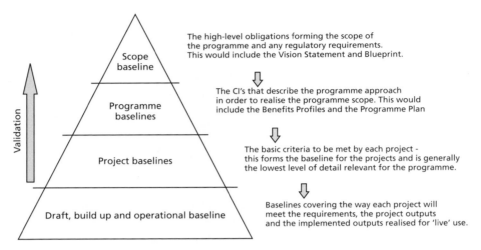

Fig. 10.2 Configuration management baseline (© Crown copyright 2003 reproduced under licence from HMSO)

Baselines exist on various levels. There could also be a sequence to the baselines whereby a higher level of detail is produced according to the results and changes realized. Figure 10.2 gives an overview of the various levels of configuration baselines for a programme. Each level of baseline within the programme serves as a reference for the underlying level.

The CIs that form the key to monitoring the programme are the scope base-lines on the one hand, and the project results on the other:
- **Vision Statement:** describes the desired outcome of the programme and is directly linked to the business strategy.
- **The Blueprint:** describes all aspects of the future situation and the associated capabilities for realizing the vision
- **The Benefits Realization Plan:** describes how, when and to what degree benefits must or can be realized. The Benefits Realization Plan is directly linked to the desired outcome(s) of the programme
- **The results of the projects and activities:** together, these deliver the capabilities needed to realize the benefits.

10.4 Quality review

Quality is not just reviewed at the end of the programme, but on a regular basis, like the progress of the programme or the level of benefits realized.

Various kinds of review can be carried out within a programme with regard to areas of quality. A review compares the end result with the programme of demands and the standards applying.

The various kinds of review within programmes each have their own character and range of application. Reviews must be planned throughout the entire programme, and it is wise to link reviews to milestones and decision points in the programme. These are often points where there is much transparency as to where the programme should be and which quality level must be complied with.

The various kinds of review are:
- *Audit:* an objective independent review of the programme as to effectiveness and execution according to agreement.
- *Review:* a formal evaluation of whether what has been delivered satisfies the pre-set conditions ('fit for use' and 'fit for purpose').
- *External scrutiny:* an external review to determine whether the programme is being carried out effectively and is delivering what has been agreed.
- *Peer review:* an internal independent review carried out by colleagues from one's own or related organization at any time during the programme.
- *Independent expert scrutiny:* an independent review by experts as to whether the programme is effective and is expected to deliver what has been agreed.
- *Gateway review:* a formal evaluation on a decision point (go/no go) in order to be sure the programme is effective and delivers what has been agreed.
- *End-of-tranche review:* a review taking place at the end of a tranche. During this review, at least the Business Case, the benefits and the benefits management process are assessed.
- *Project review:* one or more evaluations carried out after closing the project to determine whether the expected goal envisaged by the client, together with the project result, has or is expected to be realized.
- *Post-project review:* an evaluation to determine whether the pre-set goals have or are being realized. This evaluation can also be used to analyse the successes and faults in the project management process.
- *Post-programme review:* one or more evaluations carried out after closing the programme to determine whether the expected end objectives and the expected benefits have or are being realized.

10.5 Audits

As mentioned earlier, an audit is an objective independent examination as to whether the programme is effective and is being implemented according to agreement. An audit may look at specific aspects of the programme or at the programme as whole (see table 10.1). The cri-teria can be internal standards and procedures, external regulations and legislation, contract agreements, accounting standards or best practice. Audits can be carried out internally or externally, i.e. by official bodies. Auditors must inform the Programme Manager in advance as to which specific information they require. Audits can be incorporated into the programme to support the programme management.

Process	Areas of consideration for audits
Identifying a programme	Ensuring the programme fits with the business strategies and procedures
Defining a programme	Assessing alternative strategies, plans and management methods
Controlling a programme	Assessing the organization, management instruments and mechanisms
Implementing a programme	Assessing the effectiveness and efficiency of the programme implementation
Closing a programme	Assessing learning points, added value and stakeholder satisfaction

Table 10.1 Areas of consideration for audits

It is increasingly common in current practice for programme and project managers to have themselves assessed at fixed times, together with the programme or project in hand, in order to remain sharp and get as much input as possible, and thus increase the chances of success. It is no shame to make mistakes if you learn from them, and having an audit carried out helps in this regard. It strengthens the Programme Manager's position if the decision is taken to have an audit carried out regularly. These audits will then be planned on or before crucial points in the programme, and budget must be set aside for this.

Apart from management of a programme in general, audits can also be carried out on specific programme aspects such as:
• The application of risk management
• Common ground and relations with other programmes
• The use of lessons from the programme itself or other programmes
• The appraisal of options for the completion of programme goals
• Involving stakeholders in the programme and proactively representing their interests
• Emergency plans in order to be able to cope with unexpected events.

The necessary information must be collected in advance in order to carry out audits effectively. The questions to be answered are:
• What information is needed for the audits?
• How should the information be stored?
• Have the programme management processes been sufficiently documented?
• How long must the information be retained?
• How can the authenticity of the information be demonstrated?

10.6 Programme assurance

Programme assurance ensures that, amongst other things, what has been allocated to third parties will be achieved. It involves ensuring the implementation of agreed measures, updating the measures to changed circumstances, testing to see whether the measures are being carried out correctly, and seeing if they have the desired effect.

Assurance offers important added value to the programme. It gives the parties an assurance that the programme is effective, is carried out according to agreement, and is expected to deliver what has been agreed. All parties involved have responsibility for assuring that the party carries out and delivers what has been agreed, and that their own interests and those of its backers are secured. The responsibilities for this cannot be passed on to the parties to whom the work has been delegated.

Activities necessary to effect assurance can, however, be delegated to (independent) third parties. The individual parties within a programme will remain ultimately responsible at all times for their own assurance within the programme.

Assurance must, in principle, be aimed at all aspects of the programme such as:
• Quality assurance: ensuring the programme is implemented according to the Quality Management Strategy and that the elements of the programme are delivered according to the agreed quality demands
• Assuring the Business Case: that it is adequately managed and that there is always a valid Business Case
• Assuring stakeholder involvement: assuring that stakeholders are adequately involved in the programme and that optimal account is taken of the interests of those involved in the programme.

All parties within the programme have their own responsibilities in this context. The Senior Responsible Owner must ensure the programme continues to fit in with the changing business objectives and that there is always a valid Business Case for implementing the programme. The Programme Manager must ensure that all parties carry out the activities effectively and efficiently. The Business Change Manager must ensure that the programme delivers those results that will enable their own departments to realize the agreed benefits effectively, efficiently and on time.

Audits and reviews are good ways of giving form to the assurance; they can be carried out at any point during the programme.

10.7 Project assurance

Each project team is responsible for assuring the proper implementation of the project. It can be a good idea from the programme's perspective to take part, as a programme, in project reviews and project audits in order to ensure that the project continues to comply with its own Business Case and to fit in with the programme and the programme goals.

The Programme Office can often effectively represent the programme's interests at project reviews and audits. For specific and critical elements, the assurance will have to be implemented by the Programme Manager or the Business Change Managers.

10.8 Responsibilities

Overall responsibility for quality in a programme lies with the Senior Responsible Owner. The Programme Manager co-ordinates and manages implementation in everyday practice. The Programme Office will support the Programme Manager with executive tasks, such as Configuration Management and Change Control, and setting-up audits, reviews and other assurance processes.

See table 10.2 for a summary of responsibilities within quality management.

Role	Responsibilities
Senior Responsible Owner	Ultimately responsible for all aspects of quality management
Programme Manager	Drawing up the Quality Management Strategy
	Initiating and ensuring the project results in accordance with the quality criteria
Business Change Managers	Implementation, transition and realization of the benefits based on the capabilities delivered by the portfolio
Programme Office	Setting-up and maintaining the quality management activities in the programme
	Setting-up and maintaining the programme's quality assurance processes

Table 10.2 Responsibilities within quality management

Programme Management Processes

This part of the book describes the activities, the input and output, the decisions to be taken and the tasks, responsibilities and authorities throughout the course of the programme.

This part consists of:

- Overview of processes and products

- Identifying a programme

- Defining a programme

- Governing a programme

- Managing the portfolio

- Managing benefits

- Closing a programme.

11 Overview of processes and products

11.1 Introduction

The initiative to start a programme can come from any level in the organization, but it is only viable if supported by senior management. This starts with the Programme Mandate to the future Senior Responsible Owner (see figure 11.1). In order to clarify the scope of the programme, the Senior Responsible Owner will first set-up a Programme Brief (for identifying the programme) for approval by senior management (the Sponsoring Group). The Programme Mandate must include the main points of the programme objectives to be realized, as guidelines for drawing up the Programme Brief by the Senior Responsible Owner.

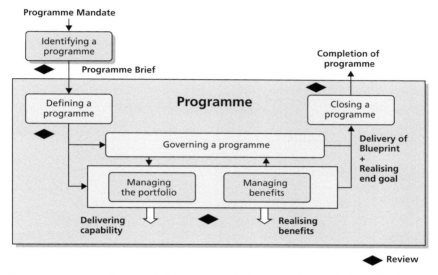

Fig. 11.1 Programme processes and main products (© Crown copyright 2003 reproduced under licence from HMSO)

The programme will be commenced after the Programme Brief has been approved, and the programme has been authorized by the Sponsoring Group. Following approval, a programme team, led by the Senior Responsible Owner and based on the Programme Brief, will prepare the Programme Definition with the associated plans and strategies for managing the programme. They will also set-up the necessary risk logs. These actions sum up what is entailed in Defining a programme.

Implementation of the programme can start following review and approval of all documents by the Sponsoring Group at the end of Programme Definition. First, programme control and a Programme Office must be set-up. The programme must be managed and the performance progress assessed throughout the entire process (programme management).

Projects must be started, and existing projects that are important for carrying out the programme must be carried out, within the context of managing the programme. The projects must be co-ordinated and phased in accordance with the diagram that states when the various benefits must be realized and adjusts for the constantly changing environment (Managing the Portfolio). The projects together deliver new capabilities based on which changes can be implemented.

The departments concerned must be prepared for the changes, and the new capabilities must be implemented. The new way of working must be embedded into the organization in order to become the new 'business as usual' and the envisaged benefits must be realized (benefits management).

The programme should be closed either once the programme goals have been achieved or if it has been concluded that the other benefits to be realized do not compare favourably with managing a separate programme organization. The programme must be given a final assessment, the organization dissolved and the remaining activities transferred to the respective departments. The responsibility for the benefits still to be realized and the associated performance measurements must be covered by the organization in the context of closing the programme.

11.2 Programme management information

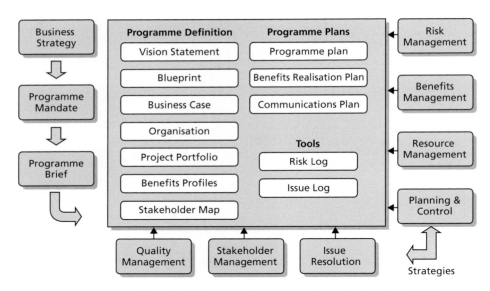

Fig. 11.2 Programme management information (© Crown copyright 2003 reproduced under licence from HMSO)

The information relevant for the programme is recorded in a series of separate documents (see figure 11.2). This information is required for managing the programme and measuring progress and performance. It is also required by the review and audit teams, who assess the process and results of the programme on behalf of the stakeholders.

The Programme Brief is the basis for setting-up the Programme Definition which includes the Vision Statement, the Blueprint, the Business Case, the organization, the Project Portfolio, the Benefits Profiles and the Stakeholder Map.

The various plans are drawn up for implementation based on the Programme Definition. These are the Programme Plan, the Benefits Realization Plan and the Communication Plan. These three plans interact strongly with one another and cannot be seen as separate.

Several strategies must be developed by programme management. These should refer to: how to deal with quality, stakeholders, issues, risks, benefits, required capabilities and planning programme management. See table 11.1 for a summary of the various documents.

The Programme Definition, the initial plans and logbooks and strategies for management are prepared during the definition process. All documents are reviewed and updated during the programme. The programme and documents are assessed during the tranche reviews and at the end of the programme.

	IP	DP	GP	MP	MB	AP
Programme Mandate	CO					
Programme Brief	CR	RV				
Outline Vision statement	CR					
Vision Statement		COM			RV	RV
Blueprint		CR	RF	UP	UP	RV
Business Case		CR	RF	RV	RV	RV
Organisation		CR	IM			RV
Project Portfolio		CR	RF	RF	RF	RV
Benefits Profiles		CR	RF	RF	UP	RV
Stakeholder Map		CR	RF	RF	RF	RV
Governance		CR	IM	RF	RF	RV
Plans		CR	RF	UP	UP	RV
Logs		CR	UP	UP	UP	RV

Com Completed
CO Confirmed
CR Created
RF Refined
IM Implemented
RV Reviewed
UP Updated

Table 11.1 Matrix programme information- and processes (© Crown copyright 2003 reproduced under licence from HMSO)

12 Identifying a programme

12.1 Context

The process for Identifying a Programme (IP) is carried out in the course of the programme, before starting the actual programme. It delivers the information required in order to justify starting a programme. The IP process is relatively short, sometimes just a few weeks.

The IP process is started with a Programme Mandate from the Sponsoring Group. It finishes with: the conclusion by the Senior Responsible Owner, the Programme Brief and the plan, the starting points for the Programme Definition phase, confirmation of these documents by the Sponsoring Group, and approval by the Sponsoring Group to start the DP process (see figure 12.1).

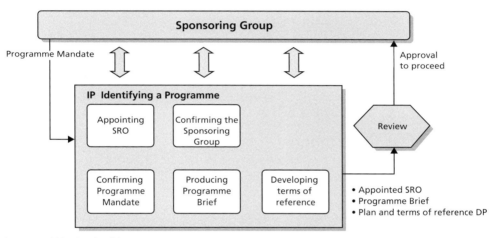

Fig. 12.1 Activities for Identifying a programme

A long process will normally have been undertaken before issuing the Programme Mandate. The Programme Mandate comes from the necessity felt by Management for carrying out changes in the organization, which might be due to threats or opportunities perceived. The need for this can be laid down in the organization's business plans leading up to the Programme Mandate. This need can, however, lead directly to the issue of the Programme Mandate.

It is essential for the programme to keep a strict eye on this need for change (which is the reason for the programme) throughout the entire process and to communicate its progress continuously within the organization. It is also essential to take note of the willingness and commitment to change with respect to senior management, the main stakeholders and the rest of the organization. The various parties' willingness to change will not be automatically in keeping with any threats and/or opportunities felt within the organization, even if the threats, opportunities, and intended changes have been put forward in the best of business plans.

Managing the stakeholders' willingness to change is an important part of the programme. The vision of the organization's future and the willingness of senior management to change, which is necessary for realizing this vision, must be ensured before starting the programme and even before starting the IP.

12.2 Basic principles

Before a programme can be started, it must be clear what must be achieved with the programme and what benefits are envisaged for the organization and the various stakeholders. Based on this, Management must be able to take the decision as to whether starting the programme is justified. It will be unwise to commence the programme if it does not fit in with the business goals or the urgency considered necessary by the organization. The programme would be doomed to fail before it started, costing money, time, energy and credibility.

Before starting the programme, it must be clear who is managerially responsible, what are the various tasks and authorities, and who are the important parties within the programme.

Finally, it will not be possible to start work on a programme unless at least the starting points and the plan for the first phase have been established. What must be delivered at the end of the definition phase and what are the standards for these documents, who does what, how and when? It is also important to establish how the main stakeholders are to be involved in the programme and how communication is to be carried out with other stakeholders during this phase.

12.3 Process description

The Senior Responsible Owner must be appointed as soon as the IP process is commenced. This person is managerially responsible for the programme and is therefore also responsible for the programme preparation process.

The Senior Responsible Owner must first of all re-confirm the Programme Mandate set, and then establish and confirm with the individual members of the Sponsoring Group their individual involvement and responsibility for the coming programme. The programme Brief and the plan for the DP must be set-up. Finally, it must be assessed to what extent the organization is in a position to realize the objectives and benefits described in the proposal.

The Sponsoring Group must confirm the outcome of the various activities within IP, approve the programme and authorize the start of the definition phase.

12.3.1 Appointing the Senior Responsible Owner

The Senior Responsible Owner is managerially responsible for the programme. He is the 'champion', the 'standard-bearer' and the 'face' of the programme. The Senior Responsible Owner must also be a member of the Sponsoring Group; preferably a leading figure in the Sponsoring Group with respect to the programme goal to be achieved, as well as being the primus inter pares.

This person is also referred to as the 'Programme Director', and within MSP as the 'Senior Responsible Owner'. The latter designation shows clearly his ultimate role and responsibility.

It is important to appoint the Senior Responsible Owner as soon as work is started on identifying the programme. The programme identification process will be without leadership unless an appointment is made and accepted. It is also essential for the programme to have a standard-bearer even in the early phase, and that the Senior Responsible Owner makes this HIS programme and gives depth to everything set-up and produced. He must be, or become, the complete owner of the programme and must play the leading role, particularly during the IP and DP processes.

The Senior Responsible Owner is often appointed directly by a Board meeting, which leads to the start of the programme and which issues the Programme Mandate.

12.3.2 Confirming the Programme Mandate

The Programme Mandate describes the strategic goals of the programme, the strategy to be followed to achieve these goals, improvements expected from these, and how the programme fits in with all the business goals, business plans and other initiatives.

This information may, of course, already be contained in a related document. It is more usual, however, that the information can only be deduced from a multitude of strategic documents produced previously within the organization. This leads to the danger that there are or will be various pictures and interpretations of what has actually been agreed.

It is therefore necessary to arrive at one coherent master document in which all aspects of the Programme Mandate are included and which describes the status of earlier documents and that they are still up-to-date on this subject. This will often require additional workshops, interviews and discussions with sponsors, members of the Management Team and other key figures. It is recommended to have the Programme Mandate confirmed by the Sponsoring Group.

It is preferable not to skip the Programme Mandate and not to proceed directly to preparing the Programme Brief. The Programme Brief is a result of the Programme Mandate. By not first confirming the current status, there is the danger that individual people might drop out in the development process. This will irrevocably lead to confusion later in the programme, as well as much wasted energy and less support within the organization.

12.3.3 Confirming the Sponsoring Group

Each programme must be supported by sponsors at the highest level within the organization; lip service is completely insufficient. Each manager from the respective departments who has final responsibility must realize his own contribution and that of his department in order to achieve the programme's end goals. He will not benefit from the programme unless the changes are implemented and benefits realized in his own department.

It is essential that all members of the Sponsoring Group remain individually, actively and positively involved in realizing the programme. They should each have their own roles and responsibilities in this regard, which they accept and to which they are committed. It can be a good idea to confirm this explicitly, publicly and individually. A publication along the lines of "Together we are strong" often works wonders.

12.3.4 Producing the Programme Brief

The Programme Brief describes the main points of the end goals as well as the improvements and benefits to be realized. The Programme Brief also states: estimates of costs and time, and the recognized uncertainties; issues; assumptions and preconditions. If necessary, the Programme Brief will state intermediate performance steps. See also chapter 22.

Much senseless and useless work is often done in a programme without a good Programme Brief. However, a thorough Programme Brief could have shown beforehand that the objectives and strategy chosen were not viable. It is therefore important to give an estimate of the costs, time and risks, etc., as well as the main goals and improvements to be achieved, in the Programme Brief.

The Programme Brief is the basis for determining the viability of the programme at the beginning. It also shows the basic information for the work to be carried out in the Programme Definition process. The Programme Brief is the basic document for communication to the respective stakeholders.

12.3.5 Developing terms of reference and plan for Programme Definition

In the Programme Definition process, the Programme Definition is prepared, the plans made for implementing the programme and the designs laid down for managing the programme. These activities in the DP must be planned in advance to ensure efficient and effective implementation. The starting points, assumptions and preconditions are laid down, based on which the plans for the work will be prepared.

What precisely must be delivered: by whom, how and when? Who will be involved, who makes the decisions and how are changes authorized (which will be irrevocable) and carried out? Will this be done by a separate team, or will the work be done essentially by the sponsors themselves? These are all questions to consider in advance.

The approach to the work in the DP will have a major effect on the costs and the duration of this phase, but will also have a considerable effect on the quality and the acceptance of the outcome. The basis for the programme will also be laid down in the DP. These are good reasons to ensure that it is right first time.

It is essential to plan the work, but even more important to establish the starting points for DP. Shall we involve the unions and middle management in the decision-making or just confront them with the outcome? How shall we process their input and who takes the final decisions? It is better to think carefully about this in advance and to communicate this effectively, than to have to alter the expectations of the various parties and win over opponents all over again.

12.3.6 Review

The Programme Brief might not be the product of a small group. It is best to have it evaluated by independent persons not involved in its preparation, even if more parties are involved.

All stakeholders should be convinced of the viability of the Programme Brief and that it is conducive to the objectives of the business. Are the defined goals realistic, do the programme objectives fit in with those of the business and are there benefits for the organization? Are the estimates realistic and have the recognized uncertainties been correctly estimated?

All stakeholders have their own responsibilities in realizing the programme and so must be able to form their ideas as to the proposed Programme.

An internal review team is normally used to evaluate this Programme Brief but sometimes an external appraisal or external review team will be used. The latter is often the case if it involves legal requirements or public interests. The Senior Responsible Owner will initiate these reviews.

12.3.7 Approving to proceed
The Programme Brief, and the starting points and plan for DP, must be finally approved by the Sponsoring Group to make the programme official. The Sponsoring Group can also authorize the beginning of DP.

Approval, however, is not automatic, and it would be quite legitimate not to approve it. The programme could draw heavily on the organization's energy, or there may be too much resistance or too little support. There may be insufficient chance of achieving the envisaged objectives and benefits. Other goals and/or strategies might fit in better with the business objectives or simply have a better chance of success.

The energy invested in IP will not be wasted if such decisions are taken. It will probably have been a good investment, as otherwise money would have been invested in the uncontrolled start of a programme, with all the associated consequences.

12.4 Input and output
See table 12.1 for a summary of the input and output of the programme identification process.

Item	Type	Notes
Programme Mandate	Input	Basis for starting the programme
		Indicates the main points of the objectives
Composition of the Sponsoring Group	Output	Appointing members of the Sponsoring Group
Appointing the Senior Responsible Owner	Output	Appointed from the Sponsoring Group
Programme Brief	Output	Basis for the decision as to whether the programme can be justified
Plans and terms of reference	Output	Describes scope, approach, capacity and terms of reference for carrying out the definition phase
Go/no go	Descision	Formal decision from the Sponsoring Group

Table 12.1 Identifying input and output in a programme (© Crown copyright 2003 reproduced under licence from HMSO)

12.5 Responsibilities
See table 12.2 for a summary of the responsibilities in the programme identification process.

Role	Responsibilities
Senior Responsible Owner	Managing development
	Preparing the Programme Brief and TOR and plans of starting points
	Managing other IP activities
	Initiating a programme review for assuring the Programme Brief (sometimes supported by a small team)
Sponsoring Group	Issuing and approving the Programme Mandate
	Appointing the Senior Responsible Owner
	Approving the Programme Brief
	Confirming the Sponsoring Group
	Assuring the programme review
	Commitment to the programme
	Issuing authorization for starting DP

Table 12.2 Responsibilities in the programme identification process (© Crown copyright 2003 reproduced under licence from HMSO)

13   Defining a programme

13.1   Context

The Programme Definition process begins following approval of the Programme Brief and authorization of the programme by the Sponsoring Group. The programme officially starts with the Programme Definition process.

The Programme Definition process is the basis for the programme. In this process, the Programme Definition is determined, the necessary plans set-up, the strategies developed for programme management and the necessary logbooks set-up (see figure 13.1).

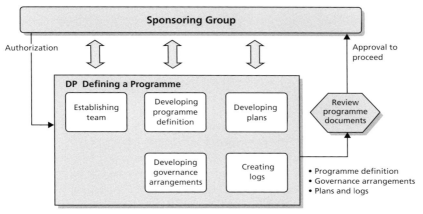

Fig 13.1 Defining activities within a programme

The Programme Definition process determines not only who does what and when, but also who is involved in the programme. What objectives must be realized, what changes must be implemented, what benefits will deliver these changes, and who is responsible for receiving which benefits and within what period of time?

A check will also be carried out to see if the necessary use of staff and resources, and the uncertainties in the programme, weigh up against the benefits to be expected. This 'Business Case' plays a key role within the programme.

On closing the Programme Definition process, the documents drawn up will be assessed in a programme review. The Sponsoring Group will finally approve the documents and authorize the start for implementing the programme.

13.2   Basic principles

To successfully realize a programme, it must be clear to everyone involved what goals must be achieved, what changes must be made for this, what benefits these changes will bring, and who has overall responsibility for this (see figure 13.2). This is an essential condition for providing direction to ensure that the people concerned accept their responsibilities and to generate support. All programmes will be doomed to fail without direction, responsibility and support.

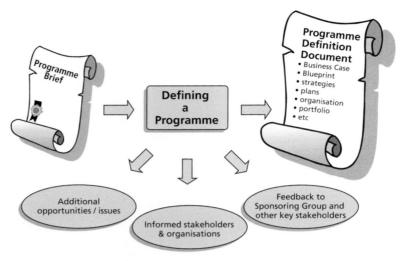

Fig. 13.2 Defining the activities of a programme

Basic documents are necessary to enable stakeholders to make a sound assessment of the necessity, feasibility and validity of the programme. Is it necessary and is it a good idea to start the programme? Does the programme fit in with the business goals? Has the correct approach been chosen, can it be financed and will the programme deliver enough or on time? Realizing a programme costs a lot of time and energy, so one should not be too rash at the implementation stage. The parties involved must be committed to the fact that investing in the programme is the best the organization can do at this point in time.

The basic documents are also needed for setting-up and implementing the programme, monitoring progress and for managing the process. Well managed programmes have a better chance of success than those that are not managed or badly managed.

The contents of the basic documents are partly determined by the environment in which the programme is implemented. Conversely, the programme and the basic documents will generate new possibilities and issues for all concerned.

13.3 Process description

It is desirable that the Senior Responsible Owner puts together a team to help him carry out the necessary work as soon as the Programme Definition phase has started.

The Programme Definition must be prepared, the strategies necessary for setting-up the management model must be developed, the necessary plans must be drawn up and the logs set-up (see figure 13.3).

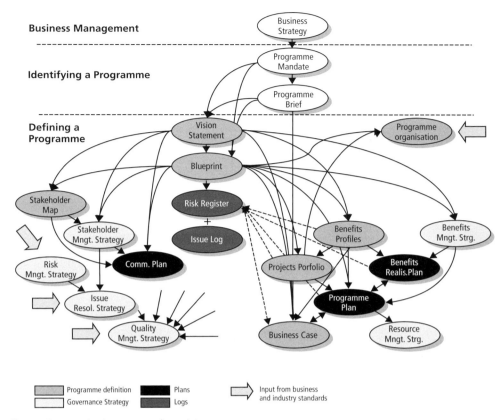

Business Management

Business Strategy

Identifying a Programme

Programme Mandate

Programme Brief

Defining a Programme

Vision Statement

Programme organisation

Blueprint

Stakeholder Map

Risk Register
+
Issue Log

Benefits Profiles

Benefits Mngt. Strg.

Stakeholder Mngt. Strategy

Comm. Plan

Projects Porfolio

Benefits Realis.Plan

Risk Mngt. Strategy

Issue Resol. Strategy

Programme Plan

Quality Mngt. Strategy

Business Case

Resource Mngt. Strg.

	Programme definition		Plans		Input from business and industry standards
	Governance Strategy		Logs		

Fig. 13.3 Programming is as pretty as fireworks!

Strategies are developed and plans drawn up from the Programme Definition. The definition, strategies and plans influence each other and must therefore be determined together.

The Risk Register and the Issue Log are required from the point where the DP process is first commenced. These documents have a key role in the DP as a register in which the recognized risks, issues and agreed countermeasures are recorded. These documents are the responsibility of the Senior Responsible Owner and the Programme Team when developing the necessary basic documentation.

The Programme Definition process delivers a wealth of products that are heavily dependent on each other. New benefits can have consequences for the Stakeholder Map, stakeholder management, the Project Portfolio, the Programme Plan, and so on; everything is interconnected. Key documents here are the Vision Statement and the derived Blueprint.

Preparing the basic documents for the programme is like fireworks, and just as interesting. See figure 13.3.

13.3.1 Establishing the team to define the programme
The Senior Responsible Owner needs his own team in this phase to help him draw up the

necessary documents, and to set-up communication with the Sponsoring Group and other stakeholders. Such a team normally consists of a few people, of whom one or two have been released to work on the programme and others work on it part-time.

The team is put together based on the terms of reference and the DP plan, as provided by IP. It is important that the team members have sufficient background, knowledge, experience and skills for carrying out their roles adequately. It is wise to have the team members trained if necessary, and joint training at the beginning of DP will also strengthen the team formation.

The team members will often fill roles in carrying out the programme. The roles that often become available are those of Business Change Managers and Heads of Programme Support. It is also recommended to appoint the Programme Manager in this phase.

13.3.2 Developing the Vision Statement

The Vision Statement describes the desired outcome from the client's perspective. It specifies the new or improved capabilities, expressed in improved performance standards, service and cost levels. The Vision Statement is derived from the Programme Mandate and the Programme Brief. Below is an example of a Vision Statement.

Example

The management of Xantix, an organization selling all kinds of margarine in the Netherlands, realizes that the business must become a European player in order to be able to deliver on time. The decision is made in the SMT to expand via internal growth. The first country for expansion is Germany. A programme is introduced with the end goal of achieving thirty per cent of its turnover in the German market within three years.

Programme Mandate and the Programme Brief. Below is an example of a Vision Statement.
The Vision Statement is a guiding document for the programme. The document gives direction and focus, and is therefore one of the most important documents for communication to the various parties involved and the basis for creating support with the stakeholders. The Senior Responsible Owner has final responsibility for, and is owner of, the Vision Statement. It is his 'State of the Union'.

13.3.3 Developing the Blueprint

The Blueprint describes the new desired situation of the organization as an outcome of the programme, including the milestones to be achieved during the programme. The Blueprint includes: a description of the organizational end situation, the new methods of working and working processes, the necessary infrastructure, and the necessary information on production, markets, management, and so on. Based on this, the new capabilities can be realized as defined in the Vision Statement (see figure 13.4).

The Blueprint is defined in the definition phase but is constantly updated while the programme is being implemented. In the definition phase, the Blueprint is often not more than a framework or an outline. Later in the programme, it becomes a detailed description of all essential aspects of the new organization.

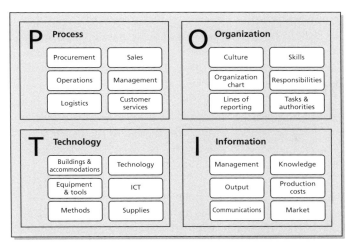

Fig. 13.4 Blueprint

The Blueprint is generally set-up by the Programme Manager, or, if he has not yet been appointed, the Programme Team supporting the Senior Responsible Owner. The Blueprint is derived from the Programme Mandate, the Programme Brief and the Vision Statement. The goals to be realized and associated benefits for the programme are the most important input for the Blueprint.

The Blueprint is used throughout the programme to maintain focus on the capabilities to be realized. There are many ways of achieving certain goals; it is essential during the programme that a consistent and coherent picture of capabilities to be achieved is available, with which work within the programme can be aimed.

Example

In the Blueprint of the Xantix programme, it is established that the necessary extra production is to be achieved by expanding the existing production line in their factory in Arnhem. Other options considered included setting up a new factory in Germany, taking over a factory in Germany, outsourcing production or increasing the existing production capacity in one of their existing factories in the Netherlands.

An eye must be kept on the Blueprint to make sure that it does not unnecessarily expand or shift during the programme to serve any other interests. This would mean the programme loses its focus, becomes inconsistent and top-heavy and finally runs aground for lack of staff, resources or financing, but more often due to the loss of support and momentum.

The Blueprint can be realized in the form of a feasibility study, which can best be set-up as a separate project. While developing the Blueprint, constant consideration must be made to the benefits to be realized, the costs involved, and enablers for their realization. It is therefore important to develop the Business Case for the programme in direct connection with the Blueprint. The initial Business Case for the programme is always a necessary result of this feasibility study.

13.3.4 Validation the benefits

The benefits to be realized are derived from the Programme Brief and the Vision Statement. It is important to further explore these benefits in the definition phase in order to arrive at a complete set of benefits to be achieved. This should include the inevitable negative effects involved in realizing the end goal.

It is essential to process these (dis-)benefits and to set-up a benefits profile for each substantial benefit. A benefits profile includes a detailed description of the benefits, and describes which capabilities must be realized to make the benefits possible, when the benefits are realized and how these must be measured.

Benefits Profiles are necessary not only for maintaining focus on the benefits to be realized, but also in order to establish who is responsible for these, what the benefits depend on, and when they must be realized. The programme will often achieve the required capabilities without this focus, but the benefits will never be realized.

The benefits profiles offer the possibility of planning, monitoring and managing the benefits. The Benefits Realization Plan will be drawn up based on the benefits profiles, which are completed and processed as necessary while the programme is being carried out.

Each benefits profile must at least establish the following:
- Description: What exactly is the added value?
- Difference: What change is noticeable before and after implementation?
- Location: Where or within which department will the benefits occur?
- Measurement: How will the benefits be measured?

Example

The Xantix programme involved the acquisition of six trucks in order to move the extra production to Germany, as current capacity is already under enormous pressure and the drivers are already doing a great deal of overtime. Without efficient monitoring of the benefits to be realized, the new trucks will be deployed in the Netherlands and a lot of money will be spent under the programme without the planned benefits being realized.

The benefits profiles are of the same order and importance for the Benefits Realization Plan as the Project Portfolio for the Programme Plan and the Product Descriptions for the Project Plans.

13.3.5 Identifying the stakeholders

All parties involved in the programme, as well their interests, must be identified early. Attention must be paid to the parties involved in realizing the programme goals, the associated benefits, and the parties for whom the programme might have negative consequences. Finally, the parties who must make a contribution to realizing the programme must be identified, as well as those parties involved in achieving this.

It is important to draw up a Stakeholder Map, including all stakeholders on one side and the various interests on the other. Such an overview provides, through its simplicity, a strong basis for setting-up the Stakeholder Management Strategy and developing the Communication Plan.

13.3.6 Designing the Project Portfolio

The Project Portfolio includes the projects and associated activities necessary for realizing the desired situation. It is directly derived from the Blueprint and the Benefits Profiles. The Programme Plan can be drawn up based on the Project Portfolio. The Project Portfolio will be completed and processed while the programme is being carried out.

On commencement of a programme, various projects and activities are often carried out that contribute to realizing the end goal of the programme. Critical activities and projects may be placed under the responsibility of the programme; projects may be joined together or adapted, And new projects will have to be initiated during the programme. All these projects must be recorded in the portfolio.

Each project description within the Project Portfolio must at least establish the following:
• Description: When will the project be started, what will it deliver and when?
• Contacts: What are the dependencies with other projects?
• Contribution: For what benefits is the project result to be delivered necessary?

> **Example**
> *The oldest production line in the Xantix factory in Arnhem must be replaced. The maintenance costs are too high and the quality of the products can no longer be guaranteed. The Head of Production has already started a project for this, which involves supplier selection. Ten new staff must be recruited for the factory in Arnhem due to the departure of some long-serving employees. The decision is taken to place the replacement of the production line and the recruitment of the new staff under the responsibility of the programme and to adapt the project and activity to the programme goal to be realized.*

The Project Portfolio makes it possible to provide a clear overview amidst the jumble of projects, various goals and directions for solutions, and several dependencies. The scope of the individual projects can be drawn up clearly and in connection with each other, and responsibilities can be established more effectively.

Fitting-in the projects with the end goal to be realized can be optimized, and conflicts between projects regarding the chosen directions for solution can be made explicit. To obtain a better overview, it is recommended that the projects and the Project Portfolio are divided into tranches.

It is not unknown that drawing up the Project Portfolio itself leads to a direct benefit by concentrating and streamlining existing projects. Projects that do not correspond to the new Blueprint will be adapted or closed, and closely connected projects will be combined. But beware the urge to place all projects in the portfolio: small projects aimed simply at maintenance and management are best kept out of the portfolio. However, it is important to ensure that these projects remain effective in the light of the larger programme. For example, it is not a good idea to paint a wall a few months before demolishing it.

13.3.7 Designing the programme's organization structure

The organizational structure for controlling and managing the programme must be planned and completed. The programme organization must be set-up in such a way that both control and management are regulated, with the necessary communication within the programme and between the programme and the business organization. The programme organization is parallel to the business organization and is often like a matrix structure superimposed on it.

The programme organization must represent the various management levels. Tasks, responsibilities and authorities, and the skills required for these, must be described for each role. The various roles must be completed, what the role involves must be discussed with those directly involved and their management, and any appointments must be approved with the green light for implementing the programme. As a derivative of this, it must be established what training is desired or necessary for the various parties involved. The programme organization can vary considerably by type of organization or programme.

For most roles, it is desirable that the persons responsible carry out the programme work as well as their own activities in the organization. It must be carefully examined to what extent the two roles conflict in responsibility or capacity. With regard to responsibility, it must be seen that the right person is in the right place. Regarding capacity, it must be seen whether a part of these activities can be carried out elsewhere or how the person can be supported in his activities. For some roles, such as that of Programme Manager, it is a good idea to hire external staff. It is also a good idea to involve the HRM and Purchasing Departments at an early stage.

13.3.8 Developing the programme's Business Case

The Business Case provides the corporate justification for the programme, based on costs, benefits, timing and uncertainties regarding the programme. The Business Case also describes the business environment and the business goals, and makes it clear how the programme fits in with this environment and these goals. It describes the 'value for money' and thus the viability of the total programme. The Business Case also contains a brief summary of the alternatives not to be implemented, together with reasons stating why not. This helps to substantiate the choice of programme and programme strategy.

The Business Case is drawn up into the programme as soon as possible (see also 13.3.3) and is continuously extended with further specification of the programme. The Business Case is updated while the programme is being implemented, particularly with regard to level transitions and major new developments that transpire.

The level of detail within the Business Case depends, among other things, on the amount of uncertainty in- and outside the programme and on the degree of monitoring necessary. It is desirable to keep the level of detail regarding costs and benefits at the same level. Very detailed cost calculations have little added value, as the benefits can only be calculated at a global level.

13.3.9 Developing the programme's governance arrangements

The method of managing the programme determines: how direction will be given to the programme during implementation, how the programme will be monitored and adjusted, how to deal with the uncertainties and new situations that will inevitably occur, and how stakeholders are to be involved in the programme. The method of management will be recorded in the programme strategies.

Benefits management

The Benefits Management Strategy describes the benefits of the programme, states where they will be apparent, and sheds light on mutual dependencies between the benefits. The strategy also describes the responsibilities for identification, planning, follow-up and realization of the benefits, and how the benefits are measured, by whom and when.

The Benefits Management Strategy is developed in close connection with that of the Vision Statement, the Blueprint and the Business Case. The Benefits Management Strategy is one of the pillars in setting-up the Programme Plan.

Stakeholder management

The Stakeholder Management Strategy describes how the programme intends to involve the various stakeholders in the programme, including how the stakeholders' contributions are to be encouraged and processed, and how feedback is to be provided on the results. It should also be established how the effect of involving the stakeholders in the programme is to be measured. The Stakeholder Management Strategy is the basis for the Communication Plan.

Risk management and issue resolution

Risks are uncertainties regarding the outcome of the programme. Issues are situations and events that are likely to affect the outcome of the programme. Risks can become issues. Issues concern the current situation and the necessary actions; risks concern possible situations and events in the future. There can be actions in order to counter or reduce a risk, or future actions if these occur or threaten to occur in the future.

The Risk Management Strategy describes how the risks are identified, analysed and evaluated. It also describes how measures for managing risks are set, how risks are to be monitored and managed, and who is responsible for this. Particular attention is given to the relations between the strategic risks, programme risks, project risks and operational risks: who is responsible for what, and how are mutual dependencies managed?

The Issue Resolution Strategy describes how issues are identified, analysed and evaluated, how measures for solving problems are set, how these solutions are monitored and managed, and who is responsible for this. As with risk management, consideration is given to links between strategic issues, programme issues, project issues and operational issues: who is responsible for this and how are mutual dependencies managed?

Quality management

The Quality Management Strategy describes how quality is ensured for all aspects of the programme. It describes the quality system, the quality assurance, quality planning and quality assessment within the programme. Who is responsible for what, and what is the necessary capacity of staff and resources for ensuring the desired quality level? What is the framework for the individual projects and activities? Who is responsible within this, and how is the quality of the outcome to be assured? How is the configuration within the programme, and within individual projects and activities, established and monitored?

Progress management

Progress management is established as a part of the Programme Plan and includes all elements of the management cycle: Plan-Do-Check-Act. This concerns both managing progress of the projects and activities, and progress of the transition, communication activities, risk activities and quality assessments. See also 13.4.

Resource management

Resource Management Strategy describes the capacities necessary for implementing the programme, where the available and required capacities for all projects are combined together over time. It highlights bottlenecks in capacity and shows how these can be solved. The capacities involve costs, resources, staff, the investments required, and technology and facilities. The strategy specifically describes staff and resources required for managing the programme. It further describes the HRM capacity necessary for supporting project management and for the transition to be implemented. Finally, the strategy describes the procedures for investment requests, procurement and financial monitoring and reporting. The Resource Management Strategy is directly linked to the Programme Plan.

13.3.10 Developing the Benefits Realization Plan

The Benefits Realization Plan can be based on the benefits profiles. This plan includes the timing that states which benefits will be realized following completion of the various project results, when 'quick wins' can be realized, and when performance steps within the programme can be realized. The plan also states when the realization of benefits within the programme will be evaluated and how realization of the benefits will be ensured on closing the programme.

It is important that the Benefits Realization Plan is prepared in close consultation with the various owners of the benefits to be realized. The Benefits Realization Plan and the Programme Plan must be developed in close connection with each other. It can be beneficial to combine both plans, but parties must beware that combining plans will mean less management consideration is given to the benefits to be realized.

13.3.11 Developing the Communication Plan

The Communication Plan is based on the Stakeholder Management Strategy. The plan includes the communication activities within the programme itself, and those from the programme to the stakeholders and from the stakeholders to the programme. The Communication Plan describes what, when, by whom, to whom, how, and via which medium communication is carried out, as well as activities for measuring the effectiveness of this communication.

13.3.12 Developing the Programme Plan

The Programme Plan is one of the central documents in a programme. The plan is based on the Blueprint, the Project Portfolio, the Benefits Profiles, the Benefits Realization Plan and the Business Case. It is also directly linked to the Resource Management Strategy.

The plan includes the cost estimate and the planning of projects and activities within the programme, the dependencies between projects, the grouping of projects in tranches, and the most important aspects of the evaluation. The plan also includes a summary of the most important risks and assumptions, the most important communication and risk management activities, quality assessments at programme level and the main transition levels. Finally, the Programme Plan includes the activities for monitoring progress and management, the necessary information, the performance levels to be achieved and the responsibilities.

13.3.13 Approval to proceed

All documents developed during the definition of the programme, such as the programme definition document, the plans, the governance arrangements and the logs, should be approved by the Senior Responsible Owner before final endorsement from the Sponsoring Group. The Sponsoring Group must give their approval to proceed together with their commitment to the investment required for the programme. This approval should be based on the successful outcome of a formal programme review.

13.4   Input and output

See table 13.1 for a summary of the input and output in the Programme Definition process.

Item	Type	Notes
Programme Brief	Input	Assessed by the Sponsoring Group at the end of the IP
Risk- and Issue Log	Output	Registering risks and issues and the respective countermeasures
Programme Definition:	Output	
Vision Statement		Describes the end goal of the programme
Blueprint		Describes the future (target) situation
Benefits Profiles		Describes the benefits to be realized
Stakeholder Map		Summary of stakeholders and interests
Project Portfolio		Summary of projects and activities
Organization		Organization chart plus description of roles
Business Case		Corporate justification
Strategies	Output	
Benefits Management		Process of identification to realization of benefits
Stakeholder Management		Process of involving stakeholders
Risk Management		Process of identifying and managing risks
Issue Resolution		Process of identification and managing issues
Quality Management		Process for quality assurance
Resource Management		Process for identification up to allocating capacity
Plans:	Output	
Benefits Realization Plan		Summary of benefits to be realized overtime
Communication Plan		Summary of communication activities over time
Programme Plan		Main points of the plan including rules on management and monitoring
Go/no go	Decision	Formal decision from the Sponsoring Group to commence implementation of the programme

Table 13.1 Input and output in Programme Definition (© Crown copyright 2003 reproduced under licence from HMSO)

13.5   Responsibilities

See table 13.2 for a summary of responsibilities in the Programme Definition process.

Role	Responsibilities
Senior Responsible Owner	Ultimately responsible for managing DP work
	Ultimately responsible for communication
	Ensuring harmonization of the programme and business planning and finance
	Managing strategic risks in the programme
	Approving strategies/management model
Programme Team	Supporting the SRO
	Developing the management model
	Drawing up plans
	Setting-up the Issue Log
Sponsoring Group	Approving the programme
	Commitment to the programme

Table 13.2 Responsibilities in Programme Definition (© Crown copyright 2003 reproduced under licence from HMSO)

14 Governing a programme

14.1 Context

Governing a programme starts as soon as implementation of the programme has been approved by the Sponsoring Group. The process includes both the setting-up of the management of the programme and the management itself.

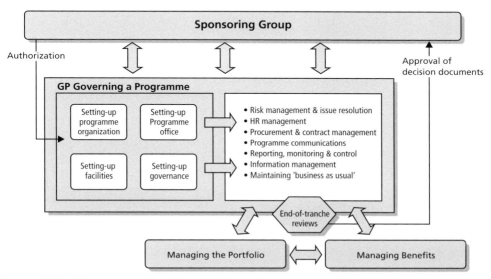

Fig. 14.1 Activities in the programme governing process

Governing the programme provides management of the programme, fitting-in the programme with the business organization, controlling the progress of projects that must deliver the new capabilities and Benefits Management that must ensure the goals and associated benefits of the programme are realized (see figure 14.1). The programme governing process is therefore the umbrella concept under which the processes of Managing the portfolio and Managing benefits are carried out.

In the case of transition between tranches, the necessary programme reviews are initiated and implemented from the programme governing process. The results of these programme reviews are submitted to the Sponsoring Group for decision-making. The Sponsoring Group decides if the programme must be continued, adjusted or closed.

14.2 Basic principles

Programmes realize major changes in the organization and always affect strategy, personnel, management, the systems and structure, and the culture. It is therefore necessary to set-up a framework within which these changes will be carried out.

The Senior Responsible Owner has ultimate responsibility for the programme. The Programme Manager is responsible for daily management of the programme. The Business Change Managers are responsible for realizing the goals and the associated benefits. Together, they form the Programme Management Team. Each has his own responsibilities for governing the programme, as well as the more operational activities directly associated with Managing the portfolio and the benefits.

On a higher level, it must be tested to see if the results as envisaged are being realized, whether the programme is being carried out in accordance with the plans, whether the programme goals continue to fit in with the business goals, and whether there is still a Business Case for continuing the programme.

14.3 Process description

As soon as the Sponsoring Group has given the green light to implement the programme, the programme will first have to be set-up and the programme organization appointed. The Programme Manager will set-up the Programme Office and ensure the primary facilities are arranged. The Programme Office will set-up the actual management structure and arrange for the remaining facilities as required.

The actual management of the programme includes reporting, monitoring and adjusting the programme, risk and issue resolution at programme level, information management, communication activities and the necessary HR and purchasing activities. At the time of the tranche transitions, the necessary programme reviews are initiated and maintained.

14.3.1 Organizing the governing process

Setting-up the programme organization

In setting-up the programme organization, the Senior Responsible Owner will appoint the Programme Manager, unless he has already been appointed at an earlier stage. The Senior Responsible Owner will ensure that the other roles within the programme are adequately filled. The individual sponsors will appoint the Business Change Manager(s) within their own departments.

For all members of the Programme Management Team, the tasks, responsibilities and authorities must be clearly agreed and laid down. On selection, it must be ensured that the individual members of the team have the correct knowledge, experience, attitude, conduct themselves in the correct manner for the roles they are to fulfil, and that they have the correct position within their own parts of the organizations. The participants will have to undergo additional training if necessary.

Setting-up the Programme Office

The Programme Manager is responsible for setting-up the Programme Office, appointing the Head of the Programme Office, and setting-up the structure for the management process. The Programme Office is responsible for providing information: collecting data, processing this and reporting on progress of the programme. The Programme Office normally provides professional support to the programme in the form of setting-up plans, budget monitoring, programme architecture and other consultancy-type activities.

 Setting-up the programme governace requirements

The Programme Office prepares the programme for the governing process, and for setting-up various support systems.

Typical software packages used in a programme are:
- Planning, estimating and budget monitoring systems
- Systems for progress monitoring such as carrying out Earned Value Analyses
- Systems for carrying out risk management, quality management and financial management
- Systems for carrying out Business Case analyses such as net present value calculations
- Configuration Management and Change Control systems
- Document management systems.

If necessary, use should be made of the existing organization's systems. However, additional systems will also have to be set-up.

Carrying out standardization of the systems over the various parties concerned is an important aspect. It is essential that projects report in a clear and uniform manner and that information within the programme is only ever generated once.

Setting-up the physical programme environment

The necessary facilities for the programme must be set-up. These include offices, ICT facilities, means of communication, transport, support software, and intranet and/or Internet website. These can be acquired from new, or procured from organizational units with one's own or associated organizations. The Resource Management Strategy states which facilities are required and how these can be procured.

14.3.2 Governing the programme

Risk management and issue resolution

Uncertainties affecting the goals to be realized and the associated benefits of the programme must be continuously monitored and managed throughout the entire programme. Bottlenecks that hinder carrying out the programme successfully must be handled adequately. It is essential that the recognized risks and issues, and the agreed management measures, are established centrally in a Risk Register and an Issue Log and are managed centrally.

Risk management and issue resolution within the programme must also assist with the risk management and issue resolution within the various projects and various departments involved.

The strategy for managing risks and issues within the programme is laid down in the Risk Management Strategy and the Issue Resolution Strategy, as set-up in the Defining a programme process.

HR management

The Resource Management Strategy includes, among other things, the procedures and necessary effort in the programme by HRM.

Programmes normally have an enormous impact on the staff's work situation, which means intensive supervision by HRM is necessary. Consultation with the Works Council and trade unions is sometimes necessary, staff must be supervised in retraining and replacement, and it is sometimes inevitable that staff will be laid off. All these changes must be supervised with the utmost care. Programmes therefore often draw heavily on the HRM's energy and a temporary reinforcement of this management is often required. It may also be necessary in the context of the envisaged changes to agree on special procedures for HRM.

Procurement and contract management

The Resource Management Strategy also includes the procedures and necessary effort for the procurement and contract management in the programme.

Programmes within one's own organization often take their toll on staff and resources, which are not always available in sufficient quantities. Normal activities must continue, as well as the programme, so it is often necessary to hire extra resources from outside to carry out and manage the programme. These could come from sister companies, subsidiaries, parent companies, or from outside. Careful selection and contracting of the extra staff is extremely important in all cases.

The procurement and contracting procedures are often directly derived from one's own organization. It can, however, be necessary to draw up additional agreements, especially for work within the programme.

Programme communication

The Communication Plan states who is informed, when, and by whom, and how feedback to and from the various stakeholders within the programme is ensured.

It is important that the parties are informed as early as possible in the programme as to the necessity for the programme, the goals to be realized, the assumed benefits, the new organization that will evolve, and the tasks, responsibilities and authorities of the people within the programme. While the programme is being implemented, they must be informed about the progress of the programme, any issues and changes, and the benefits already realized and still to be realized.

Reporting, monitoring and control

Periodic reporting on the progress of projects and the benefits realized is necessary in order to maintain an overview of the progress of the total programme.
Issues must be identified and, if necessary, escalated, and corrective measures taken in order to keep the programme on schedule.

It is important to ensure that the organization's new status to be realized (the Blueprint) remains internally consistent, and is consistent with the goals to be achieved. It is therefore necessary that the Programme Manager and the Senior Responsible Owner remain appropriately informed over the status of the programme, and have the authority and opportunity to adjust this if necessary, without an overload of information and without them assuming the management of individual projects.

Information management

The various programme documents should be developed further while the programme is being implemented and updated. This must take place at the end of each tranche and before the programme review takes place, but preferably more often. Regularly updating the Blueprint makes it possible to carry out necessary amendments in the Project Portfolio. The Programme Plan and the Benefits Realization Plan must also be updated in order to show the current state of progress and to adjust this as necessary.

End-of-tranche reviews

The programme Business Case, the benefits realized, and the benefits management process must be evaluated at least at the end of each tranche in a programme review. Such a review will assess what has been realized, what is yet to be realized, and whether this is realistic and fits in with the objectives within the programme.

The programme review is also used to see whether the programme is efficient and effective enough and complies with the previously defined Programme Definition, plans and strategies.

At least one programme review must be planned after the programme has been closed to ascertain whether the benefits within the respective departments have been realized as envisaged.

Maintain 'business as usual'

It's business as usual while renovations take place. If it's not, when the operation is over, the patient will have died.

The new working methods and services must continuously fit in with the existing operational management. The transition from old to new must be carefully planned, which requires management at the highest level within the programme, as well as harmony between the programme and business units involved.

14.4 Input and output

See table 14.1 for a summary of input and output in the programme governing process.

Item	Type	Note
Programme Definition	input	For setting-up and governing the programme
Programme Plan & Benefits Realization Plan	input	For monitoring the progress
Strategies	input	For setting-up and governing the programme
Communication Plan	input	Plan for carrying out communication activities
Risk Register	output	Registering risks and management measures
Issue Log	output	Registering issues and the agreed actions
HR and procurement standards	output	Must satisfy business standards
IT and other facilities	output	For supporting the programme
Progress reports	output	Progress reports on all programme elements regarding the plans
End of tranche reviews	Descision	Programme evaluation with regard to strategic objectives

Table 14.1 Input and output in the programme governing process (© Crown copyright 2003 reproduced under licence from HMSO)

14.5 Responsibilities

See table 14.2 for a summary of the responsibilities in the programme governing process.

Role	Responsibilities
Senior Responsible Owner	Appointing the Programme Manager
	Ensuring the other roles within the programme are adequately filled
	Communication with key figures
	Managing the most important strategic risks
	Managing the Programme Manager and Business Change Managers within the programme
Programme Manager	Setting up the programme governing process and the Programme Office
	Monitoring and managing progress according to plans and the Business Case
	Updating the key programme documents
	Ensuring internal and external consistency of the programme
	Risk and issue resolution at programme level
Business Change Managers	Ensuring 'business as usual'
	Providing input for the reviews
Programme Office	Setting up procedures for governing the programme
	Setting up facilities for governing the programme
Sponsoring Group	Appointing Business Change Managers

Table 14.2 Responsibilities in the programme governing process (© Crown copyright 2003 reproduced under licence from HMSO)

15 Managing the portfolio

15.1 Context

Within a programme, Managing the portfolio involves managing the projects and connected activities within the programme that together produce the new capabilities necessary for realizing the programme goals (see figure 15.1). The existing and the new capabilities together deliver the Blueprint for the new organization.

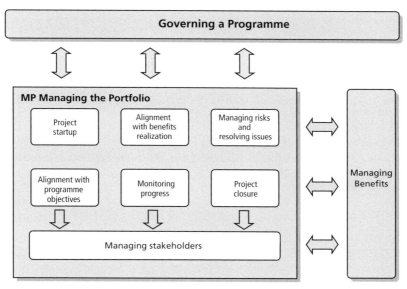

Fig. 15.1 Activities in the portfolio management process

Managing the portfolio includes the daily co-ordination of projects and activities for managing the programme as a whole, as defined in the programme governing process.

Managing the portfolio is directly linked to the benefits management process. The output from Managing the portfolio, i.e. the capabilities, is the direct input for the benefits management process. Both processes must therefore be closely geared to one another in order to enable effective realization of the programme goal and associated benefits.

15.2 Basic principles

Daily co-ordination is needed between the various projects and activities within a programme to ensure that there is, and remains, internal and external consistency between the results of these projects and activities and the capabilities they must deliver.

15.3 Process description

There will be projects within the programme that were already in existence, as well as projects that will need to be started within the framework of the programme. In the portfolio management process, the existing projects must be brought under the programme governing procedure. New projects and activities must be initiated, and both new and existing projects should be aligned with the programme goals and benefits to be achieved.

The progress of the projects must be monitored and adjusted if necessary. The risks of the projects for the programme and vice versa should be managed and bottlenecks solved. Projects must be delivered and transferred to the business units to realize the goals and associated benefits. Lessons from projects that have been closed will also benefit current projects and those yet to be started.

15.3.1 Project startup

The Programme Manager is responsible for starting new projects and activities, and must ensure suitable team members are appointed such as the Project Executive, the Project Manager, and any other members of the Project Management Team.

Background	Context leading up to the project
Project definition	Project goals, scope, outcome, definition, preconditions and relations with other projects
Main points of Business Case	Describing how the project contributes to the programme goals, in measurable units if possible
Quality expectations	What aspects are important for the outcome to be delivered
Acceptance criteria	The values regarding quality that must be realized
Risks	Recognized risks important to the project
Main points of project plan	The first indication of the costs and time or desired completion date

Table 15.1 Contents of Project Brief

The Programme Manager must make sure that the responsible team members know what has to be delivered, when and within what budget, what the programme aims to achieve with the project result, how the project is to be realized, and what agreements have been made within the programme regarding the use of staff and resources.

The Programme Manager, together with the Project Executive, must harmonize tolerance levels and make agreements about within which framework the project result must be delivered. The Project Team must reach agreements with regard to money, time, scope, quality, benefits, deployment and risks with regards to accepted deviations from the project plan.
 Procedures must be established regarding the quality assurance and project management, go/no go while carrying out the project, the reporting structures, Configuration Management and Change Control, risk management and the escalation procedure.

The Programme Manager will issue a project mandate before starting a project. The Project Team draws up the Project Brief (see table 15.1). The project initiation document (PID) is drawn up following approval of the Project Brief. Implementation of the project can be commenced after the PID has been approved.

15.3.2 Aligning projects with programme objectives

Existing projects of strategic importance for the programme must be brought under the management of the programme.

The PID of a project must be assessed for consistency with the programme. The project must be adapted if necessary to fit in with the capabilities to be delivered, as defined in the Blueprint, the Programme Plan and the Benefits Realization Plan.

15.3.3 Aligning projects with benefits realization

The Business Change Manager is responsible for ensuring that the benefits relating to individual projects are realized after the project result is delivered. The Business Change Manager must also be sure that the project enables this, as described in the Project Brief and later in the PID. During implementation of the pro-jects, the Business Change Manager will ensure that the projects continue to deliver what he needs for fulfilling his own responsibilities. The Business Change Manager will have to adapt the benefits profiles and the Benefits Realization Plan where necessary.

15.3.4 Monitoring progress

The Programme Office must support the individual project teams in developing the project plans and defining the reporting structures. The same templates should preferably be used for planning and reporting throughout the entire programme.

The progress of each project must be monitored against each project's plan. Each departure from the agreed project plan must be assessed for consequences for the rest of the programme. Consequences for other elements of the programme must be identified and assessed as soon as possible in order to react quickly to the departure.

The project status should be assessed for:
- Results to be delivered: do these still satisfy the demands placed on them by recent users?
- Timing: was the outcome delivered on time? Does the completion fit in with other projects and/or the planned transition and benefits realization?
- Costs: have the estimated costs been exceeded? The costs have a direct influence on the Business Case to be realized
- Scope: changes in the scope can have dramatic consequences for the project itself, and for the rest of the programme.
- Benefits: what are the expected benefits envisaged with the outcome to be achieved?
- Staff and resources input: both the use of personnel and the results of resources and financing.
- Risks, issues and starting points: projects in a programme are often heavily dependent on one another, often involving major risks. Issues must be dealt with immediately. Differences in starting points can lead to unpleasant surprises later.

15.3.5 Managing risks and resolving issues

Programmes will never be carried out entirely to plan. The environment is always changing; delays occur, starting points and opinions change, and new threats transpire. It is therefore important that the Programme Manager keeps a finger on the pulse regarding uncertainties that might affect the programme. Actions must be taken to react to new issues. The Programme

Manager must escalate to the Senior Responsible Owner uncertainties that are greater than expected. The Senior Responsible Owner has final responsibility for the programme and thus for the risk and issue resolution of the programme.

15.3.6 Project closure

On closing projects, the project result must be delivered and transferred to the programme, and by the programme back to the business units to realize the goals and benefits envisaged. The completion is the starting point of the transition of the outcome into the business organization, and the beginning of implementation of the planned changes.

It must be ensured on completion that the recommendations for follow-up actions in the Lesson Learned Report have been prepared. The recommendations contain all issues that might be of importance in the user phase, such as training, as well as changes not yet implemented and additions. The Lesson Learned Report includes all the recommendations that might be of use for current and future projects. The Programme Manager is responsible for ensuring that the recommendations for follow-up actions and the Lesson Learned Report reach the right parties.

It is not possible to assess directly on delivering a project whether the final benefits generated with the project still weigh up against the costs. This can usually only be assessed if the outcome has been in use for some time. Only when the benefits to be realized are in sight is it wise to carry out an objective review. A similar post-project -review may be fitted into the schedule of programme reviews, as agreed earlier.

15.3.7 Managing stakeholders

The management of the stakeholders is very important for the success of the programme. The co-operation and support from the stakeholders will be received only if the stakeholders are well informed about the programme, have a good understanding about the progress and have the feeling that their individual interests are respected.

Also a good and open communication between all members of the Programme Management Team is vital for the success of the programme.

All information should be reliable, accurate and up to date. The Communication Plan defines the communication activities to be carried out.

15.4 Input and output

See table 15.2 for a summary of the input and output in the Portfolio Management process.

Item	Type	Notes
Project mandate	output	For starting projects
Project Brief and Project Initiation Document	input	For authorizing the beginning of the project or the beginning of the implementation of the project
Project progress reports	input	Reports on the main points and phase- and project end reports
Project result	input/output	The delivered outcome of the project
Lesson Learned Report	input/output	For improvement of current and future projects
Benefits Profiles	input	Highlighting on ascertaining and adapting the scope of the projects
Benefits Realization Plan	input	Updating as a result of continuing projects
Blueprint	input	Updating as a result of delivered project results
Issue Log	input	Recording issues and measures to resolve them
Risk Register	input	Recording issues and countermeasures
Programme Plan	input	Updating and specifying as required by the projects; the transition plans must also be updated
Business Case	input	Updating and evaluating as a result of project results
Communication Plan	input	Basis for communication activities

Table 15.2 Input and output in the Portfolio Management process (© Crown copyright 2003 reproduced under licence from HMSO)

15.5 Responsibilities

See table 15.3 for a summary of responsibilities in the Portfolio Management process.

Role	Responsibilities
Senior Responsible Owner	Monitoring progress on the strategic level
	Advising the Programme Manager
	Solving bottlenecks
	Ensuring commitment by the Sponsoring Group and other key figures
Programme Manager	Starting, co-ordinating and closing projects and activities
	Monitoring the progress of projects and activities at programme level
	Updating the Blueprint, portfolio and plans
	Informing stakeholders as to progress made
	Managing stakeholders' expectations
Business Change Manager	Ensuring the projects deliver what is necessary for implementing the changes
	Planning transitions
	Ensuring 'business as usual'
Programme Office	Ensuring the programme documentation system
	Supporting projects and the programme
	Collecting information/updating documentation
	Giving advice and reporting progress
Project teams	Delivering the project result to the programme
	Project progress reports
	Harmonizing with Programme Office

Table 15.3 Responsibilities in the Portfolio Management process (© Crown copyright 2003 reproduced under licence from HMSO)

16 Managing benefits

16.1 Context

Managing the benefits includes the entire phase of identifying the benefits, up to and including implementing the changes. It also includes realizing and measuring the added value resulting from carrying out the programme. Managing the benefits comes under managing the programme as a whole, as defined in the governing the programme process (see figure 16.1).

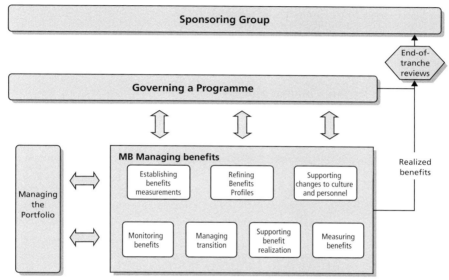

Fig.16.1 Activities in the process of managing the benefits

Managing the benefits is directly linked to the process of Managing the portfolio. The output of Managing the portfolio, i.e. the capabilities, is the direct input for the process of managing the benefits. Both processes must therefore be thoroughly co-ordinated with one another to enable effective realization of the programme goal and the associated benefits.

16.2 Basic principles

Actually realizing the individual benefits is a responsibility of the respective sponsors and business departments. This involves them taking responsibility from their individual positions in the business for the entire process of identification, from the moment when the implementation of the programme has been approved up to and including realization and measurement of the benefits.

This responsibility within the programme lies with the Business Change Managers. The Business Change Managers within their own departments are responsible in this context on behalf of their sponsors, and within the programme on behalf of the Senior Responsible Owner. Here, the Business Change Manager will consult with and work very closely with the Programme Manager.

The departments have their own responsibilities in this regard as early as the phases for identifying and Defining a programme. This responsibility is described in both phases, and is therefore not part of the process for managing the benefits.

16.3 Process description

Managing the benefits commences with ascertaining the method of measurement and the current situation (baseline measurement). The benefits must be monitored and the Benefits Profiles refined and updated while the programme is being implemented. Are the forecasted benefits still considered relevant as a new situation? Can new benefits be identified? Will other forecasted benefits no longer apply?

Following completion of the projects, the results must be implemented, the changes carried out, and the achieved benefits measured.

16.3.1 Establish benefits measurements

The current extent of the performance must be clear in order to measure the benefits of the changes to be implemented. It is therefore essential at the beginning of the programme to carry out a baseline measurement. This baseline measurement might already have been carried out during the programme, in the definition phase, or directly on commencing implementation.

The method of measuring the benefits is also defined with the baseline measurement. This shouldn't be taken lightly; it is important to define values that are reasonably independent of environmental factors or other improvements realized. Benefits can sometimes be easily measured as a financial result of a certain activity. At other times, a combination of values will give insight into the improvement, for example, a combination of Economics (cost reductions to be implemented), Efficiency and Effectiveness (the three Es). For benefits that are difficult to quantify, such as customer and employee satisfaction, a combination of indicators can be set with a derived financial basis.

It is important to establish the relevance of the indicators in advance and to agree on these with the parties. Go further into what the various indicators mean if the programme environment changes during the programme. See what the enablers are, meanwhile, to be able to measure the various indicators. The enabler that is charged against a performance measurement must be taken into account in relation to the added value of the benefit for the organization.

16.3.2 Refining the benefits profiles

The Benefits Profiles must be further processed and updated during the programme. They must constantly show the latest status of the benefits in the programme.

The level of detail of the Benefits Profiles should correspond to the level of detail of the costs of the enabler in realizing the benefits. Costs and benefits are of equal importance to the programme. There is therefore no point in calculating the cost to two decimal places, if the benefits can only be calculated and converted into large units.

16.3.3 Monitoring benefits

Throughout the entire programme, the progress must be measured with regard to the Business Case, the Programme Plan, the Blueprint and the Benefits Realization Plan.

An important aspect of monitoring the programme is monitoring the benefits to be realized. Are the benefits to be realized still valid or not? They may change considerably: they could increase, disappear completely, or change into dis-benefits by changing circumstances. Some important reasons for changes in the benefits are: alterations in the sponsors' business organizations; changes in the plans to be implemented based on lessons from earlier projects; environmental factors and changes in the programme goals.

16.3.4 Transition management

The business organizations must implement the project results into operational management, in order to implement the envisaged changes. This must be prepared in order to ensure that the changes can be carried out and that normal operational management (business as usual) can also be continued. The changes can be implemented in one go, or in a series of small steps.

The work that needs to be carried out for implementation is laid down in the Transition Plan, the main points of which are already contained in the Programme Plan. The Transition Plan is refined and updated before the last tranche transition. It is approved on authorization of the tranche in which the transition takes place, and the effort invested by staff and resources finally approved. Separate Transition Plans are also prepared for separate imple-mentations.

16.3.5 Support changes to culture and personnel

Implementing changes often requires much consideration by individual members of staff. Changes in an organization's strategy, structure, management, organization, systems and infrastructure nearly always have consequences for the use of personnel and the culture of the organization. Programmes therefore often have an important role set aside for HRM.

16.3.6 Supporting benefits realization

Actual realization of the benefits is carried out by the operational business units. The Business Change Manager is normally only the facilitator in this, and not the actual manager with operational responsibility. He may be operationally responsible for some elements, but very rarely for them all as this is not necessary. However, for the other elements, he must facilitate realization of the benefits, in which case he will represent the business manager with final responsibility (sponsor) within this business unit.

16.3.7 Measuring benefits

The Benefits Profiles define the benefits to be realized. The method of measurement and the baseline measurement have already been dealt with. The final link in the chain is measuring the benefits realized and comparing them with the goals. This is carried out periodically or with the programme reviews, depending on the benefits and the method of measurement. Some benefits are less suited to periodic measurement and are only measured at the end of a tranche at the programme review.

16.4 Input and output

See table 16.1 for a summary of the input and output in benefits management.

Item	Type	Notes
Benefits Profiles and the Benefits Realization Plan	Input	For establishing the measurement method for performance and realizing benefits
		For carrying out the baseline measurement
		For performance measurements and establishing the benefits achieved
Benefits Management Strategy	Input	Defines the entire process of realizing and establishing benefits
Business Case, Blueprint, Programme Plan, project progress reports	Input	For optimizing projects, managing the transition and monitoring the realization of benefits
Performance improvements and realizing goals and benefits	Output	Measured improvements as the outcome of implemented improvements
Issue Log	Input	Establishing issues and measures for their resolution
Risk Register	Input	Establishing risks and countermeasures
Communication Plan	Input	Basis for communication activities

Table 16.1 Input and output of benefits management (© Crown copyright 2003 reproduced under licence from HMSO)

16.5 Responsibilities

See table 16.2 for a summary of responsibilities in benefits management.

Role	Responsibilities
Senior Responsible Owner	Ultimately responsible for realizing benefits
	Ongoing advice and management
	Ensuring continuous commitment from the Sponsoring Groups and other key figures
Programme Manager	Carrying out activities in the context of risk and issue resolution in order to prevent or minimize obstacles getting in the way of successful realization of the benefits
Business Change Manager	Managing the transition and implementation of project results in normal business operations
	Implementing changes
	Realizing the benefits
Programme Office	Refining and updating the benefits profiles
	Collecting information for realizing performance and benefits
	Reporting progress with regard to the Benefits Realization Plan

Table 16.2 Responsibilities in benefits management (© Crown copyright 2003 reproduced under licence from HMSO)

17 Closing a programme

17.1 Context

The process for Closing a programme is the last in the procedure. It completes the other processes such as Governing a programme and Managing the portfolio and benefits. The projects will normally already have been closed; the realization of the benefits will be transferred to the individual business units and the programme closed.

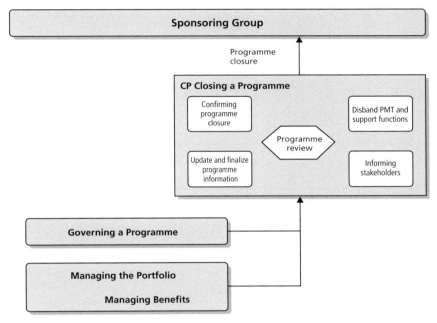

Fig. 17.1 Activities involved in closing the programme

The Blueprint for the new organization is thus achieved or, in any case, one or more quality steps in the process and certain benefits will have been realized. Other benefits may still need to be realized or increased further before the final goal of the programme has been completely fulfilled. Managing the realization of the remaining benefits is transferred to the business units involved.

The process for Closing a programme can also be initiated by a decision to close the programme early, arising from new developments or new opinions in the organization.

17.2 Basic principles

A programme will not end by itself. It must be consciously closed as soon as it is decided that the added value of realizing the goals via the programme is less than the energy and effort by management that it costs to maintain it. There may be more important goals that justify this energy and management effort.

Programmes could run for years and even become a set feature of the organization, if they are not consciously closed. The singular business organization would then, in parts, become a matrix organization.

17.3 Process description

The stakeholders will be given confirmation that the programme is to be closed. The final programme review will be held, the programme documents closed, the programme organization dissolved, and the Programme Manager and Senior Responsible Owner discharged.

The stakeholders in this context can be either those persons involved with the end result of the programme and/or those providing the use of staff and resources.

17.3.1 Confirming programme closure

A programme can be closed as soon as the last project has been delivered, the project result has been implemented into the business organization, and the new capabilities according to the Blueprint have been completely integrated into the respective business units.

Following closure of the programme, the realization of benefits must be continued, and even extended, to continue to achieve the programme's end goals. This will require securing the support of the respective business units, and making provisions to ensure that measuring the benefits is continued.

It often takes years before the new way of working becomes 'business as usual' with no possibility of returning to old habits and ways of working. This can take longer than the (already long) duration of the programmes themselves. It is therefore essential for the realization of the end goal and benefits to be firmly embedded in the business organization itself, and that the necessary support for this is regulated for business management.

Confirmation of the programme closure involves: formal confirmation that the Business Case has been fulfilled; support for realization of the end goal and agreed benefits regulation after the programme; that all remaining activities from the programme have been transferred to the respective business units.

If a programme is closed prematurely before the Blueprint has been entirely realized, the current projects still underway must be transferred to the business management of the business unit that is most involved, or to other programmes. Projects not being transferred must be closed.

17.3.2 Programme review

A formal assessment takes place at the end of the programme to establish whether all capabilities as defined in the Blueprint and all agreed goals and benefits have been realized. It will establish whether the programme has been effective and been carried out according to agreement. The assessment will also look at what lessons can be learned from the programme and whether these can be of value for other programmes.

The review can also include a scrutiny by external parties, for example, from the parent company, government, or other official or political body.

One or more assessments can be carried out after the programme has been closed to see whether the agreed goals and benefits have been or are being realized. The original Senior Responsible Owner normally heads such post-programme assessments. A point for evaluation in such an assessment is how far the respective business organizations are in a position, and have the 'drive', to continue implementing the agreed improvements, or whether internal and external circumstances have changed to the extent that this ambition is no longer appropriate.

The post-programme assessments are planned during the programme. They are, however, no longer part of the programme.

17.3.3 Updating and finalize programme information
The programme documents must be cleared out, updated and archived for possible future assessments. All outstanding risks and issues must be concluded or transferred to the respective business units.

17.3.4 Disband Programme Management Team and support functions
The programme organization must be dissolved. The suppliers of staff and resources must be informed; people must finish their work with the programme and responsibility for their efforts must be transferred to the respective business unit. This sometimes involves personnel having to return to the workplace they had before being deployed in the programme. This requires the necessary supervision and must be carefully planned in advance. Many people working on the programme will have experienced personal growth in the course of it, which makes placing them back in their old positions undesirable.

The Programme Office must be dissolved, facilities dismantled, and offices cleared. Contracts for personnel, products and services must be terminated or transferred to the respective business units.

The Senior Responsible Owner will discharge the Programme Manager. The Sponsoring Group will discharge the Senior Responsible Owner.

17.3.5 Informing stakeholders
The Senior Responsible Owner and the Sponsoring Group will confirm closure of the programme to the stakeholders and point out what the programme has achieved. They will also inform the stakeholders about how to proceed. How can the respective business units secure the end goal and the benefits to be realized after the programme has been closed?

17.4   Input and output
See table 17.1 for a summary of input and output in the process for Closing a programme.

Item	Type	Notes
Programme documentation	Input	Cleared out, updated, formally closed and archived
Confirmation of programme closure	Output	Official confirmation to the stakeholders that the programme is being closed
Programme review	Output	Assessment of the programme itself and the realized goals and benefits
		Planning future reviews to be held as business as usual
Lessons and programme assessment	Output	For the benefit of future programmes

Table 17.1 Input and output in the process for Closing a programme (© Crown copyright 2003 reproduced under licence from HMSO)

17.5 Responsibilities

See table 17.2 for a summary of responsibilities in the process for Closing a programme.

Role	Responsibilities
Senior Responsible Owner	Heading the programme review
	Discharging the Programme Management Team
	Endorsing the programme closure
Programme Manager	Finalizing the programme documentation
	Dissolving the Programme Management Team
	Clearing or releasing facilities
Business Change Manager	Measuring performance and benefits realized
	Investing the benefits in the line
	Investing performance and benefit measurement in normal business operations
Programme Office	Concluding programme documentation
	Archiving for possible future reviews
Sponsoring Group	Confirming programme closure

Table 17.2 Responsibilities in the process for Closing a programme (© Crown copyright 2003 reproduced under licence from HMSO)

Annexes

This part of the book contains the following annexes:
- Other methodologies
- Roles of the Programme Management Team
- Performance measurement methods
- List of definitions
- Organization of management products
- Literature list
- Reference list
- Contact addresses
- Index.

18 Other methodologies

18.1 Change methods

There are many different methodologies based on changes. In this chapter, a number of these methodologies will be compared with MSP. A distinction is made between the elements requiring attention on implementing changes and the steps to be taken to achieve the changes, i.e. areas of attention and approach.

Weggeman recognizes six elements that are important for change within an organization. OGC, De Caluwé, Lewin, Kotter and Wijnen have defined steps in implementing changes. Tuckman and Graves indicate development phases in team formation, in which parallels can be seen with phases of change.

18.2 Weggeman

Projects and programmes are often used by organizations to give structure to change processes. Nowadays, changes in organizations are the order of the day, but they often cause unrest in the organization. Methods and techniques offering structure to the change process can be used to give as much chance as possible of success. In the book "Ondernemen binnen de onderneming", Weggeman[8] recognizes six elements that are important for a change within the organization (see figure 18.1):

1. Strategy
2. Personnel
3. Management
4. Systems
5. Structure
6. Culture.

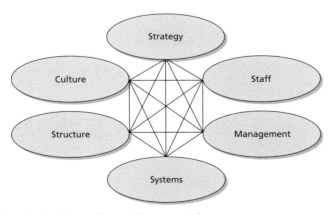

Fig. 18.1 Elements of organizational changes (source: Weggeman 1985)

These six elements are important in any business and cannot be considered independent of one another. Changes in one element will have consequences for all other elements. In a change process, classification according to these elements gives the process something to hold on to. One can see for each element what effect the changes have had on the organization, and this can also give an insight into the change and increase the chances of success.

18.3 How to manage Business Change

OGC has developed and published other methodologies, as well as MSP. One of the least known of these is the methodology "How to Manage Business Change"[9], which also fits in entirely with the MSP method.

"How to Manage Business Change" by OGC (2001) describes a 'process of change' in which a change is implemented in eight steps. On closer consideration, these steps appear to be a wake-up call for the reader to want to prepare for the change. The change is actually implemented between steps 7 and 8, followed by a review in step 8 to ascertain the extent to which the new situation corresponds with the desired situation (as described in the Blueprint). Figure 18.2 shows the OGC change process.

This change process shows a cycle from defining the reason via ascertaining the initial situation, the desired end situation, and the steps in between. It ensures the capability for the organization in order to change, the most appropriate approach, and the manner in which the goals can be achieved according to the review of what has been achieved in the meantime.

Fig. 18.2 Change process (© Crown copyright 2001 reproduced under licence from HMSO)

18.3.1 Step 1 - Reason

Fundamentally, consideration is given to the reason for the change. It is much easier for people to accept that things change if they know why this is necessary. The people involved can also place the change in context if they know the reasons for it. Changes involve much uncertainty, so it is crucial to communicate the certainty that exists as efficiently as possible. A SWOT analysis (strengths, weaknesses, opportunities and threats) can be the reason for initiating a change. Such an analysis could show that there are either opportunities for a business that it cannot pass by or threats that cannot be ignored. This understanding of opportunities and threats will give a feeling of whether or not to start work with such a situation in the short or long term. People refer to the 'pain' felt by an organization in this situation. This may give rise to a sense of urgency which determines how the change is handled and what priority it is given.

OGC refers to a "pain/gain matrix" whereby the level of impact for the organization is marked out against the level of simplicity of implementation (see figure 18.3). This shows a rough priority classification from "Why bother at all" to "Take forward as quickly as possible".

18.3.2 Step 2 - Actual situation

This step deals with getting a good picture of how things are now. This is also called a baseline measurement or an ACTUAL situation. A SWOT analysis (strengths, weaknesses, opportunities and threats) is a good way of providing a picture of the actual situation. Such an analysis will show what the organization is good at, what can be improved, what the chances are for the organization, and what the threats are if it proceeds on the path it has embarked upon. The analysis will give rise to the feeling of necessity for possible changes. This is referred to as the "pain" experienced by the organization in the current situation. It will give rise to a "sense of urgency" that determines whether changes must be implemented and, if so, how and what level of priority will apply.

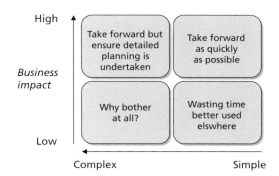

Fig.18.3 Pain/gain matrix (© Crown copyright 2001 reproduced under licence from HMSO)

18.3.3 Step 3 - Desired situation

From this picture, a comparison can be made with the desired future perspective. The desired situation or TARGET situation is described in MSP, the Vision Statement and the Blueprint, which show an unambiguous and clear picture of the situation after the change. Here, it is important to ensure a clear outline (scope) for what must and must not happen, and the advantages this will deliver for the organization.

18.3.4 Step 4 - Necessary change

By analysing the difference between ACTUAL and TARGET situations, it is possible to establish what must be done and a plan can be made for implementing the changes: how to proceed from ACTUAL to TARGET. This corresponds in MSP with the Programme Plan. A first Business Case can be prepared, based on the details collected so far.

18.3.5 Step 5 - Ready for change

Once it is clear where the organization stands and what the proposed situation is for the future, it is important to see whether the organization also has everything 'in-house' to deal with the change. The next step contains the central question "Is the organization ready for change?" Here, consideration must be given to preconditions such as sufficient resources and the correct infrastructures (for example IT or logistics aspects), and cultural and emotional aspects also play a role. Is the organization willing to change in order to make a success of it? It may be that not everyone thinks its interests are best served by the change.

The term 'culture' is also described as 'the way we do things here'. Culture consists of unwritten rules, the organization's own history, a system of values, norms and balances of power. The stakeholders in the change are part of the organization and share the same culture. There can sometimes be a conflict of personal and business interests, and it is a good idea to have a clear picture of what you can expect of a stakeholder, or that you can derive unexpected or different behaviour from this.

Before proceeding to the next step, the Change Management Team must be convinced that the organization is ready for change, or that this will be achieved in the short-term where this is not the case.

18.3.6 Step 6 - Approach

The approach chosen for implementing change in the organization is determined, among other things, by the necessary speed, the impact of the change for the organization, the level of co-operation in the teams, and the willingness to change. OGC recognizes the following classification for changes:
* Transformation changes: all changes are implemented in one go; also called the "big-bang" scenario
* Incremental changes: the change is more gradual with this approach, according to an evolutionary process
* Modular changes: the changes are divided up and carried out in smaller more manageable tranches.

18.3.7 Step 7 - How to achieve this

Whichever steps are chosen to realize the change, whether the colour green, yellow, red, white or blue as a point of view is chosen, the question still remains as to how to achieve the change in practice. A professionalization phase in a government organization will require a different approach than in an advertising agency, but one will still have to look for a number of similar pillars in order to achieve and assure the change in the organization. If only knowledge is transferred, this will soon slip away, and an organization under pressure will return to the 'old' ways. Knowledge can be more efficiently applied by supplementing the transfer of knowledge with supervision, thus changing skills. This way, the new way of working will be maintained for longer and it will take more time or pressure for the 'old' ways to return. The change will last if the choice is made for a combination of knowledge transfer, supervision, and assurance in the organization. The organization has the knowledge in-house for demonstrating the new behaviour, the supervision for its application, and the assurance from the organization to continue doing so.

18.3.8 Step 8 - Review

The last step in the OGC change process is the review, which involves looking back on the change. What was the TARGET situation and where is the organization after the change? There might be some elements of the change that must still be carried out or that have not entirely had the expected effect. These points can be the impetus for a new change cycle.

18.4 Colour classification according to De Caluwé

In the book "Learning to change" by De Caluwé[10], use is made of a colour print classification with which the changes are typified. Using the colours yellow, blue, red, green and white, each colour has its own characteristics and special approach. The most important question with this classification is: "Things/people will change if you ...".

Yellow (thought based on yellow) deals with power and interests. The starting point is that an organization will change if, for example, interests are combined and the parties are forced to adopt various viewpoints. The key point is that the person effecting the change must continuously take account of the collective interests, parties and stakeholders, and must be capable of making negotiations and conflicts productive. This type of change process is difficult to foresee. Groups of stakeholders will often be brought together to contribute their interests collectively.

Thought based on blue proceeds from a rational approach whereby the changed situation is developed and people go from A to B based on a well thought-out, step-by-step plan. Arguments and facts or figures are of primary importance in determining the solution. Thought based on blue proceeds from a "world of feasibility". Individual summaries are of less importance, and the processes can be planned accurately and are relatively short.

The 'soft side' of change management is summarized in thought based on red. This way of thinking is very much based on human resource management, the starting point of which is stimulating people to change either by way of sanction or bonuses. This is a question of perception, and it is important that something be given back if people give something. Enforcing this, however, as is possible with blue, has many limitations here. This type of change process costs a lot of time. The processes can be successful by setting goals, motivating their achievement and making them attractive.

Green processes are characterized by action learning. Making the organization aware of the new way of thinking or its own shortcomings will produce the challenge to change. A person effecting the change will provide motivation by outlining the prospect of learning new things. The duration of green processes is highly dependent on the learning capacity of the organization and the people in it. Whereas, in the case of red, there was still some time to enforce things, this is absolutely forbidden with thought based on green, as it is highly counter-productive. The person effecting the change is more of a supporter than a manager; creating permanent groups is very effective.

Finally, there is the white approach. Thought based on white proceeds from the fact that people and organizations are themselves continuously changing. This deals with self-organization with a certain degree of predictability, and no co-ordinating structure to show what must happen and how. Motivation, own energy, and space for the individual workers or groups are determining factors in the change, which can only be governed if desirable at that point in time. The person effecting the change is there purely in a supporting role to remove barriers and to clear or solve conflict situations.

All of these methods can be used to approach changes, or they can provide input in determining the most suitable approach. The method of change chosen will determine the attitude of the person effecting the change, the changes to be made if this involves intervention, and so on. Various colour approaches can appear alongside one another within a programme.

18.5 Unfreeze-change-refreeze by Lewin

Lewin[11] refers to another approach, that of unfreeze-change-refreeze. He discovered that people are naturally opposed to changes; there is resistance to change that is automatically seen as a threat. The greatest delaying factor with changes is caused by resistance to disruption of the established positions of power and interests, particularly if this disruption is due to pressure from above or outside.

The person effecting the change must be determined to prevent and intercept resistance when announcing the change, thus making the organization more amenable to it. The change can then be implemented and become a solid part of the organization's structure by ref-reezing. The structures within the organization will serve as starting points for new changes. The change process will only succeed if the entire cycle has been concluded and new balance found. The unfreeze-change-refreeze cycle is iterative and must be followed continuously.

18.6 Team formation according to Tuckman and Graves

There is great risk involved in introducing change at the point when it is announced. Announcements of mergers and takeovers often lead to storms of protest and resistance caused by fear and uncertainty. What does this mean for me? What will my position be?

Team forming, according to Tuckman[12], is carried out in four steps:
1. Forming: by bringing the team together and determining the right to existence as a group and individually
2. Storming: to determine the power struggle for priority between individuals
3. Norming: rules are determined
4. Performing: team results are booked and co-operation gets underway.

Graves[13] has a similar classification for team development, but refined in more detail (see figure 18.4).

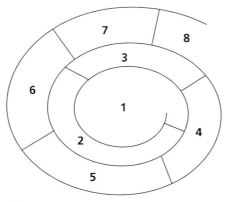

Fig. 18.4 Team forming according to Graves

The formation of teams (and therefore also new organizations) goes through all the steps one by one, which are also expressed in colours. In step 1 (beige), all the people who are to form the new team are brought together. The group will first ask itself: "Do we have a right to exist?" "What is our contribution?" The next step will be taken if agreement exists as to these questions. In step 2 (pairs), the central question is: "Do I belong here?" Each individual will want to feel part of the team that is to be formed, even though the group itself has a right to exist.

In step 3 (red), there is a power struggle in order to decide the hierarchy within the group. "Who are the 'heroes' and where do you stand on the informal ladder?" This step is very important for the future. The opinions and results of the following steps will be greatly influenced by the distribution of power that takes place. Step 4 deals with laying down internal rules and agreements: "The way we work". This will provide structure to what must be done.

There has been no reference to a team until now. These individuals were charged with forming a team together, but it is very important to give such a group the chance of proceeding through these stages together.

Step 5 (orange) is characterized by its result orientation. The first outlines of a team become visible and the first joint results realized. This is an important step in forming the team. Work is carried out on mutual trust and trust in the team, making the move to step 6 (green) easier. In this stage, a team is formed and co-operation entered into to achieve results. This is the stage that most businesses are currently in.

The last steps are 7 and 8. Step 7 (yellow) is still quite rare in practice and stands for integration and external orientation. The team has thus reached such a level of co-operation that it acts as one integral unit. Step 8 (turquoise) indicates utopia, a stage in which everything and everybody works in harmony. No organization is known to be in a state of harmony.

Team formation goes from step 1 to as far as the team can in the development stage. It is also possible for teams to be combined in various stages; this will always lead to a new team being developed and starting together from step 1. In the case of mergers, resistance always seems to occur, as management wants to achieve this faster than the staff. Where management has been involved for months in the preparation of such a process, and they come together in exactly the same manner, the staff is not involved until a later stage of the change. The announcement of a merger or takeover is normally only made once all agreements have been concluded (step 4) and co-operation can be commenced (step 5/6). The staff does not get the chance to make the first step in the team forming process until the announcement has been made, and will not be ready for co-operation, while management wishes to embark on the next step.

If Change Management understands this, resistance can be intercepted.

But how is a team phased out? This is actually very simple. Each team that breaks up goes through the same steps but in reverse order i.e. from the point of team development back to step 1. This should be accounted for when putting together the programme organization and when dissolving the team on Closing a programme.

18.7 The eight steps of Kotter
In 1995, Professor J.P. Kotter[14] (Harvard University) defined eight steps for changes within organizations:
1. Establishing the need for the change
2. Forming a strong Sponsoring Group
3. Setting-up a vision
4. Communicating the vision
5. 'Empowering' management in implementing the changes
6. Realizing 'quick wins'
7. Embedding improvements into the organization and realizing additional improvements
8. Institutionalizing the new way of working.

The steps defined are by nature both preparatory (step 1 up to and including 3) and executive (step 4 up to and including 8).

The fact that many of these methods have been developed from practice is apparent from the vision of changes by Gert Wijnen. Much agreement can be seen between the change processes described by Wijnen and Kotter.

18.8 The change process according to Wijnen
Wijnen15 characterizes the change process as five steps undertaken successively:
1. Realization
2. Determining the position and developing a vision
3. Building up support
4. Realizing the change
5. Embedding this into the organization.

These five steps are carried out during each stage of the change. Each change will cause 'pain' in the organization and can take place anywhere, at any level within the organization. The pain is caused by a difference between the desired and the existing situation. This leads to the need for change towards the desired situation.

Step 1 in the change process is becoming conscious of this need, up to the level of responsibility within the organization. The second step, determining the position and developing the vision, must deliver a deepening of the need in step 1. Change for the sake of change only leads to unrest; but change driven by a clear and supported vision can deliver energy. For this, the vision and strategy of the change will have to be embedded into that of the organization, and the need for the change explained clearly. This process will often deliver a number of concrete plans for improvement and points for short-term profit. In the third step, the change must be emphasized more within the organization, the main reasons being support and involvement. This step is also the period in which it is a good idea to realize the first results of short-term profit, which will help create wider support within the organization.

Support can be created by allowing the workers involved to be part of the change process. This is possible in various ways, for example, by helping in the thinking and decision processes. Key figures must be involved in an early stage if a change is to have a good chance of success. Key figures or 'heroes' are those who are seen by the staff as being in authority. They can be found in all positions, on all levels, and include those persons who have the trust of the staff but no real authority from the hierarchy.

In the 'realization of the change' step, there is support in the organization and it is clear what must still happen. Now is the moment to implement the definitive changes. This will generally be given structure and form by the projects. An improvement cycle can also be used for this purpose; think about the Deming- circle (Plan-Do-Check-Act).

The last step is embedding the change into the organization. This involves actually applying the new situation into everyday practice (see figure 18.5).

Fig. 18.5 Embedding changes into the organization (source: giggle cartoons).

Here, the benefits that were the reason for the change must be realized. The result of the change is directly dependent on support in the organization for the new situation. There will be considerable negative effects if staff does not see the advantage of working with the new methods and it is therefore important to involve the staff, or users in MSP terms, as early as possible in the change in order to promote acceptance.

18.9 MSP and the change methods

Table 18.1 shows a summary of the OGC, Kotter and Wijnen processes compared with the MSP processes.

MSP	How to manage business change	Kotter	Wijnen
Identifying a programme + Defining a programme	Reason	Sense of urgency	Realization
	Actual situation	Vision and strategy + Forming Management Team	Determining position + Developing a vision
	Desired situation		
	Necessary situation		
	Ready for change		
	Approach		
	How to achieve this		
Governing a programme + Managing the portfolio + Managing benefits		Communicating	Building up support + Realizing changes
		Support	
		Quick wins	
		Consolidation	
Closing a programme	Review	Embedding into the organization	Embedding into the organization

Table 18.1 Comparison of MSP, "How to manage Business Change", Kotter, and Wijnen

Each step in the change process brings the organization closer to the change, and each situation must be considered individually as to how this can best be completed. It is important to maintain understanding that every method is a guide and not a guarantee for success. Each situation requires its own conscious interpretation.

Seen from the colour perspective as described, for example, in the book "Learning to change", the MSP method is strongly 'blue' oriented when it comes to the rational approach, where the changing situation is developed and the new situation is worked towards based on a step-by-step plan. On the other hand, the method strives towards space for individual parties within the programme, in order to arrive, based on an outline and one's own authority, at one's own interpretation of that outline. Here, the method makes a fundamental distinction between people responsible for implementing projects and activities that deliver a certain outcome and those responsible for transition and embedding the new method of working into the existing organization. MSP emphasizes that one's own approach and way of handling this are required within the various areas of the programme in order for the programme to succeed. You could imagine MSP producing a framework in which management can take place according to various colour styles.

Changes within organizations, and everything connected with these, are very complex and the methods used to ensure success are diverse.

Change management is an art in itself.

8   Ondernemen binnen de onderneming, Mathieu Weggeman and others
9   How to manage change, Office of Government Commerce
10 Learning to change, Leon de Caluwé and others
11 Resolving social conflicts; selected papers on group dynamics, Kurt Lewin
12 Developmental sequence in small groups, Bruce W. Tuckman
13 Levels of Existence: An Open System Theory of Values, Clare W. Graves
14 Leadership in change, John P. Kotter
15 Projectmatig Werken, Gert Wijnen and others

19 Roles of the Programme Management Team

19.1 Sponsoring Group

The Sponsoring Group represents senior managers responsible for investment decisions. It decides the direction of the programme and the framework ventured into in order to achieve the desired goals.

The Sponsoring Group has the following responsibilities:
- Delivering the Programme Mandate and the investment decision
- Creating an environment in which the programme will prosper
- Stimulating, advising and supporting the Senior Responsible Owner
- Continuously demonstrating loyalty and support for the programme and the Senior Responsible Owner
- Approving the progress of the programme regarding the strategic goals
- Showing leadership and loyalty to the programme during communication events
- Confirming successful completion and endorsement on closing the programme and discharging the Senior Responsible Owner.

19.2 Senior Responsible Owner

The Senior Responsible Owner has final responsibility for the success of the programme.

The following are particular responsibilities of the Senior Responsible Owner:
- Being the owner of the vision and the 'champion' of the programme
- Ensuring the investment, for the definition and the implementation of the programme, and the transition activities so that the desired benefits will be realized
- Giving direction and leadership throughout the entire programme and bearing personal responsibility for the outcome (this would be an important performance measure for the individual functioning of the Senior Responsible Owner)
- Responsible for overall governing of the programme by ensuring that the programme and the necessary investments are set-up and managed according to suitable processes and procedures of sufficient quality
- Responsible for key programme documents including the Programme Brief and Business Case
- Managing the interface with the most important stakeholders and ensuring effective interfaces and communication with the stakeholders
- Managing the most important strategic risks within the programme
- Ensuring consistency of the programme with the business goals and strategies. Business goals will continue changing and issues will continue to arise. It is the responsibility of the Senior Responsible Owner to ensure that issues continue to be dealt with correctly
- Ensuring that the organization and personnel are carefully supervised during the change, and that the results are analysed and evaluated objectively and lessons learned implemented whenever necessary

- Initiating and heading evaluations, both during the programme and following its closure, for evaluating whether the programme:
  - is consistent with the goals to be realized
  - delivers what has been agreed
  - delivers the benefits agreed
- Controlling and supporting the Programme Manager.

The Senior Responsible Owner requires the following skills:
- Clear vision
- Ability to ensure investments
- Ability to give objectives and direction to the programme
- Strategic decision-making abilities
- Leadership by example
- Maintaining focus on the programme's end goal
- Ability to build up productive relations within the Programme Management Team
- Gaining the trust of the major stakeholders
- Ability to make decisions based on various sources of information
- Ability to chair meetings of the Programme Management Team.

19.3   Programme Manager

The Programme Manager is responsible, on behalf of the Senior Responsible Owner, for general programme management and realizing new capabilities, particularly those laid down in the Blueprint.

More specifically, the responsibilities of the Programme Manager are:
- Developing and planning the programme and pro-actively monitoring its progress, solving issues and taking appropriate corrective measures
- Defining the roles, processes and procedures for governing the programme
- Ensuring the integrity of the programme; internally oriented to consistency within the programme and externally oriented to consistency with infrastructure planning, other programmes, and general technical and specialist standards. These responsibilities are sometimes allocated to a single role (often under the denominator 'design architect'), in particular with long and complex programmes
- Monitoring the programme budget on behalf of the Senior Responsible Owner and evaluating expenses and costs compared with output realized during the programme
- Facilitating appointment of the right persons within the project teams
- Ensuring that the completion of new products and services by projects satisfies quality demands, time and budget, in accordance with the Programme Plan and agreements made in the context of governing the programme
- Ensuring maximum effectiveness when deploying resources and staff within the Project Portfolio
- Managing contributions from third parties to the programme
- Managing communication with stakeholders
- Managing relations and dependencies between projects
- Managing risks to ensure successful completion of the projects

- Initiating extra activities and other management interventions with the goal of ensuring progress of the programme and solving issues
- Regular consultation with the Senior Responsible Owner on the programme's progress.

Programme Managers require the following skills:
- Effective leadership and interpersonal and communication skills
- The ability to command respect and create a group feeling under the managers of the project team
- Good knowledge of planning, evaluating, monitoring and adjusting programmes
- Good knowledge of project management methodologies such as PRINCE2
- Knowledge of programme management methodologies such as MSP
- Good knowledge of budgeting and procedures in the area of resource planning
- Sufficient seniority and acceptance for advising project teams on their projects with respect to the programme
- Ability to find solutions and prevent problems.

19.4 Business Change Manager

The Business Change Manager is responsible to the Senior Responsible Owner for identifying and defining the benefits, monitoring progress and achieving the benefits defined.

The following are particular responsibilities of the Business Change Manager:
- Ensuring the programme completes the interests of the Sponsoring Group
- Ensuring for the Sponsoring Group that the new capabilities provide maximum support in realizing the benefits envisaged
- Working with the Programme Manager to ensure that work within the programme, including the scope of each project, covers all aspects necessary for delivering the capabilities needed to realize the benefits
- Working with the Programme Manager to identify projects that could contribute to the benefits to be realized and the goals to be achieved
- Identifying and defining the benefits and making sure the goals and the benefits of the programme are also realized
- Identifying and implementing maximum improvements in existing and new business operations when delivering the project results to the business units
- Managing realization of the benefits and ensuring benefits can be continuously developed and measured after the programme has been completed
- Establishing and implementing mechanisms to ensure benefits are realized and laid down
- Assuming leadership in implementing the project results, ensuring 'normal business operations' is continued during the changes and that these are implemented effectively and integrated into the business management
- Preparing the respective business units for the new ways of working in order to be able to implement the new business processes ('unfreeze')
- Optimizing the timing of the delivery of the project results to the business units concerned.

The following skills are required of Business Change Managers:
- Detailed knowledge of the business environment
- Knowledge and experience in the field of change management

- Sufficient experience for creating order in complex situations
- Keeping an eye on programme goals
- Knowledge and experience in the field of change technologies (for example, Business Process Re-engineering (BPR))
- Knowledge and experience in the field of benefits identification, modelling and management techniques.

19.5 Programme Office

The Programme Office is responsible for technical and administrative support of one or more programmes.

The following are particular responsibilities of the Programme Office:
- Recording and reporting performance measurements and process
- Information management:
  - managing all baseline documents for the programme
  - generating all necessary programme information
  - managing, controlling and updating the programme documentation
  - setting-up and managing the index in an electronic library of programme information
- Financial reporting:
  - supporting the Programme Manager by way of budgeting monitoring and budget reports on the programme
  - managing the status reports for all projects in the programme
- Recording and monitoring risks and issues:
  - analysing relationships and critical dependencies between projects and advising the Programme Manager as to the required measures
  - managing the Stakeholder Map
- Quality control: recording of mutually consistent ways of working and standards that fit in with the agreements made on programme management, such as project planning and reporting, change control and risk management
- Change Control:
  - establishing changes for periodic checks and results
  - monitoring measures agreed
  - ensuring actions are carried out on time
  - reporting on whether actions agreed have been carried out (on time) or not.

Additional responsibilities of the Programme Office may include the following:
- Delivering a strategic summary of all programmes and elements, and reporting on these to senior management
- Providing 'consultancy' support to project teams while initiating and implementing the project and ensuring a joint approach and 'best practices' are adopted
- Carrying out evaluations and giving advice on implementing improvements during the cycle of the programme and the individual projects (for example, arranging workshops for the project teams, stakeholders and members of the Project Management Team).

Programme Office staff require the following skills:

- Thorough experience of programme and project management and their implementation in organizations
- Expertise in programme and project management methods and techniques
- Relevant experience in risk management
- Skills in the area of operational management and business evaluation
- Interpersonal and communication skills on all levels.

20 Performance measurement methods

A number of methods can be used to measure the performance of a programme. This does not involve evaluating the progress of a programme and what went well or less well, but assessing the degree of the success of the programme. Some of these methods are explained below.

20.1 Balanced Scorecard

The Balanced Scorecard (BSC) has become a widely used method in recent years as a structured way of providing a summary of various performance measurements, as seen from the point of view of various stakeholders. A BSC views performance from four perspectives (see figure 20.1):
- Financial: how was the financial performance (mainly used for shareholders)
- Primary processes: which internal processes contribute to customer and shareholder satisfaction and must therefore be excellent
- Innovation and growth: how the capacity to change is improved in order to arrive at the vision that has been set
- Client: how is work done for the client in order to arrive at the vision that has been set.

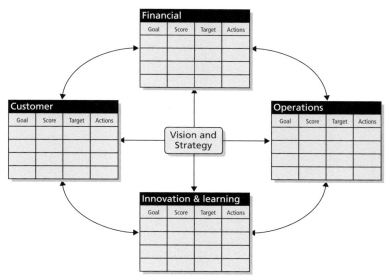

Fig. 20.1 Balanced Business Scorecard

The BSC helps to find the balance between striving for short and long-term goals, and is based on the organization's strategy and vision.

20.2 Benchmarking

Benchmarking is a common marketing tool. It is used to mark out one's own organization or department against comparable entities in the environment. This gives a picture of how one's own organization operates so that possible improvements can be envisaged.

Benchmarking can be specifically used for:
• Objectively assessing performance
• Exposing points for improvement
• Testing to see if improvements have been successful.

Comparisons can be carried out in various ways. Benchmarking uses comparisons of standards, results and processes.

20.3 EFQM Excellence model

The EFQM Excellence model gives structure to strategic improvements and makes it possible to measure these improvements. The advantage of this model is that it use general terminology that is recognizable and suitable for all sorts of businesses where comparison of processes and methods of working is possible. This model is sub-divided into nine areas, and uses five enablers and four result areas (see figure 20.2).

Enablers refers to all factors that can be assessed as to whether the organization has the capabilities to realize the strategic improvements. These are points of consideration by the managers when governing the organization. The enablers are:
• Leadership
• People management
• Policy and strategy
• Resources
• Processes.

On the other hand, there are measured results that must be marked out against the norms and the trends. The results to be measured are:
• People satisfaction
• Customer satisfaction
• Impact on society
• Business results.

By feedback from the results to the enablers, it is possible to work on improving the organization's innovation and learning capacity.

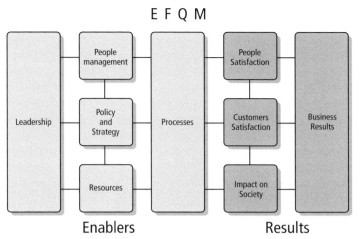

Fig. 20.2 INK model

20.4 Goal Question Metric

The Goal Question Metric (GQM) technique uses a division according to:

- Products
- Processes
- Resources.

This technology is based on the assumption that all elements can be linked to goals. By way of questions, the organization's performance is assessed for each area or the quality of that area. The questions are linked to standards and the answers are quantitative by nature.

The basis of this technology is that goals must be defined and linked to norms in order to measure performance. There must also be a structure enabling comparison of the quantitative answers with the norms and goals.

21 The MSP Examination Scheme

Introduction

Within the field of project and programme management, qualifications are becoming increasingly important. Individuals find examinations a straightforward way to demonstrate their level of competency. More importantly organisations gain great benefit form adopting a standard approach. Examination qualifications are a cost effective and rigorous way of assisting staff to operate in a consistent way. Furthermore if an organisation adopts an examination based standard, they can more easily recruit staff who hold suitable relevant qualifications. Furthermore this principle can be extended from individuals to vendors. So if an organisation wished to engage a vendor they can require potential partners to only put forward staff who hold the relevant qualification.

OGC recognised the value of an independent and widely available qualification when they updated their project management method PRINCE to the PRINCE2 standard in 1996. At that time they introduced the foundation and practitioner qualifications in PRINCE2. Many readers will be familiar with these exams therefore in this chapter we will compare and contrast the PRINCE2 and MSP exams.

Readers who are not familiar with the PRINCE2 exams should, however, not be concerned. There is no requirement for those sitting MSP exams to have any knowledge of PRINCE2.

Examination Body

Only APMG can offer MSP examinations. The APM Group (www.programmes.org) was founded in 1993 as a trading arm of the Association for Project Management. It became an independent organisation in 2000.

APMG provides examinations via two routes - public centres and via Accredited Training Organisations (ATOs). Exams are offered at a single public venue in England at about two monthly intervals. Details are available on here:
www.programmes.org/Web/Site/MSPQualifications/OpenCentreExams.

Accredited Course Providers

The vast majority of MSP qualifications are sat as part of a training course. These courses can only be provided by ATOs. The training material management systems and trainers of ATOs are regularly assessed to ensure that their training courses attain an appropriate standard. At the time of writing there were nearly thirty ATOs. The full listing of ATOs can be found here:
www.programmes.org/Web/Site/TrainingOrganisations/ATOListing

Availability

Public exams are held at approximately two monthly intervals. Places are limited and bookings should be made with APMG well in advance.

ATOs can run exams any week of the year at any venue for clients, although they must book exams several weeks in advance. While ATO's can run abbreviated courses for clients who have undertaken an element of self study, they are not licensed to provide an examination only service.

ATOs also run a wide range of open courses that individuals can attend. Open courses run every week of the year somewhere in the United Kingdom with one ATO or another. These run less frequently in other countries, but open MSP courses have been run around the world. Arrangements can also be made for the British Council to invigilate exams overseas.

Qualification Scheme

There are three MSP qualifications. These descriptions of the examinations are taken from the syllabus:

Text in italics is © The APM Group Ltd 2005. It should not be reproduced without the express permission of The APM Group Ltd.

Foundation

The Foundation Examination tests the general understanding of the fundamental principles of MSP based on the book. This is intended for those who intend to work within a programme environment, who need to know the terminology used and some of the theory behind the practice. It is also the start point of providing a higher level qualification.

Format

The Foundation Examination is closed book with short answer and multi-choice questions to the value of 50 marks, to be answered within 45 minutes. Pass mark will be 50% (25 correct answers).

Intermediate

The Intermediate Examination requires a comprehensive understanding of the principles and theory of the MSP book. This is intended for someone coming into programme management perhaps (although not necessarily) from project management and as a stepping stone from the concepts to the higher level of understanding. It is also anticipated that anyone wishing to move into other roles within programmes would be able to achieve this qualification thereby helping them to gain the relevant theory and understanding.

Format

The Intermediate Examination is closed book with a choice of three from five questions requiring written answers within 90 minutes with 20 minutes of reading time at the beginning during which the examination paper may be annotated. Additional material in the form of reports, formats, statements, scenarios, etc. may be provided with some examination papers set.
The pass mark is 50% (38 marks out of a possible 75)

Practitioner

The Practitioner Qualification is intended for programme managers demonstrating an excellent understanding in the principles and theory of the MSP book supported by practical application and a good general level of understanding that comes from having worked within large programmes. The pass mark is 50% (38 marks out of a possible 75)

Format

The Practitioner Examination is open book with one compulsory question of several parts to be answered within 90 minutes with 10 minutes reading time at the beginning during which the examination paper may be annotated. This will be based on a complex scenario which will be issued at the time of booking the examination and which should be used to work on during the training course for this examination. Additional material in the form of reports, formats, statements, scenarios, etc. may be provided with some examination papers set. Other material in the form of course notes, examples, copies of presentations, etc. can be used during this exam but no electronic aids, such as laptops, may be used.

The pass mark is 50% (38 marks out of a possible 75)

Comparing the three MSP Examinations

Before we look at each MSP examination, it will be useful to look at the relationship between the three examinations.

The Foundation Examination tests the candidate's basic knowledge of MSP. The Intermediate Examination tests whether the candidate can apply MSP in a theoretical way. Finally the Practitioner Examination tests if the candidate has applied MSP in a practical sense in programmes. Or if they have sufficient experience of programme like situations that they can imagine how they would apply MSP in a real world situation.

Some of this flavour comes through in the following extract from the syllabus with gives the learning outcomes at each of the three levels for one of the seven MSP principles

Syllabus Unit BM - Benefits Management

Overview

This unit provides a guide to the effective management of benefits from the initial definition and objectives through to the realisation and review of them at the conclusion of a programme. It provides examples of benefits modelling and the necessary processes that must be used to ensure effective benefits realisation.

Unit Content

Overview of Benefits Management

1. The main reasons and objectives for benefits management
2. The importance of effective benefits management within different programme and business situations

The Benefits Management Process

3. *The identification of the required outcomes and the development of the necessary framework for the management and realisation of benefits.*
4. *The development of a Benefits Management Strategy*
5. *The identification of benefits including the differing types, their potential origins and their interrelationship*
6. *The modelling and quantification of benefits*
7. *The responsibilities for benefits management*

Benefits Realisation

8. *The development of benefit profiles and the benefits realisation plan*
9. *The reviewing of benefits realisation*

Learning Outcomes

Following completion of this unit you will know how to undertake the following activities. These are listed under the three examination levels to highlight the increasing levels of competence you will need to demonstrate in order to achieve the required standard.

Foundation

1. *Describe the fundamental importance of the benefits focus of programme management*
2. *Describe in outline the contents and their importance of each the following documents in relation to the overall management of benefits: Vision Statement, Blueprint, Benefits Profiles, Benefits Realisation Plan, Benefits Management Strategy*
3. *List the factors that should be considered in the development of the Benefits Management Strategy*
4. *State which of the following benefits-related deliverables are input to or output from each of the MSP programme processes: Benefits Management Strategy, Benefits Realisation Plan, Benefits Profiles.*
5. *Describe the typical benefits management activities of the Senior Responsible Owner, Programme Manager and Business Change Manager(s) for each of the MSP programme processes*

Intermediate

6. *All the competences listed above for the Foundation level.*
7. *Describe in detail the relevance, importance, production, usage and transformation of benefits-related deliverables in and by each of the MSP programme processes based on a given scenario*
8. *Describe the benefits management activities undertaken by all relevant roles for each programme process based on a given scenario*
9. *Describe and explain the interfaces between Benefits Management processes and deliverables and all other relevant areas of MSP*
10. *Describe and explain the use of Benefits Management in the re-evaluation of a programme's viability based on a given scenario*
11. *Describe and explain the use of Benefits Management as an input into the Business Case and the Financial Plan for a given scenario*
12. *Develop a typical Benefits Management Strategy, Benefits Management Plan and Benefit Profile from a given scenario*

Practitioner

13. *All the competences listed above for the Foundation and Intermediate levels.*
14. *Define, develop and explain in detail examples of Benefits Management in action relating to examples of a Vision Statement, Blueprint, Benefits Management Strategy, Benefits Management Plan, Benefits Profiles, or the equivalent documents, with explanations of their relative strengths, weaknesses and lessons learned based on personal experience and related to a given complex scenario*
15. *Use Benefits Management to define a programme's early wins, tranche structures, project objectives and programme dependency network*

Comparison with PRINCE2 Examinations

The MSP syllabus again provides a useful, initial insight into the relationship between the MSP and PRINCE2 examinations:

The Managing Successful Programmes (MSP) book provides guidance on the principles, processes and tools to use to manage programmes in any environment. It is necessarily less detailed and prescriptive than the equivalent for projects (PRINCE2) and, at its highest level, demands much more of the practitioner. With this in mind, this syllabus reflects the need for those who wish to gain qualifications in MSP, to demonstrate increasingly higher levels of competence.

The relationship between the PRINCE2 and MSP examinations can be stated more simply:
- The MSP Foundation Examination is similar to the PRINCE2 Foundation Examination
- The MSP Intermediate Examination is similar to the PRINCE2 Practitioner Examination
- The MSP Practitioner Examination has no equivalent in the PRINCE2 arena.

The Foundation Examination
Prerequisites

There are no formal pre-requisites for this examination. Practically it is also not necessary to have any experience of programmes before sitting the Foundation Examination. This book does provide sufficient information for the studious reader to sit and pass a Foundation Examination. But most students find it difficult to simply read a book and then sit an examination. There are also now several computer based training packages available, which again require a high level of student discipline.

Preparation for the examination

On the other hand, most students find about three days of training is a comfortable and enlightening way to reach foundation standard. We therefore recommend that anyone with a significant involvement with a programme being run under MSP should attend a foundation level training course and sit the Foundation Examination.

Candidates for the Foundation Examination should not be unduly worried at the prospect of sitting an examination. The multiple choice format means the answers are in front of the candidate and the Examination Board is under a remit to set the Foundation Examination at a level where the vast majority of candidates will pass.

Most candidates need do no more than try a few sample papers and read their training notes and the MSP manual or this book.

Hints and Tips during the Examination

There are a few simple disciplines that will, during the Foundation Examination, help the candidate avoid some simple mistakes. Common mistakes are:
- Failing to read the question and possible answers in full and thoroughly
- Rushing difficult questions and then getting subsequent questions wrong because the candidate is still thinking about the previous question
- Changing answers from right to wrong.

The best approach is to:
- Cover subsequent questions with a blank piece of paper
- Carefully read one question
- If the question is complex or contains negatives, recast each possible answer as a statement and ask if it is right or wrong
- Only put an answer on the answer grid if certain it is correct
- If unsure which answer is a correct, mark incorrect answers on the question sheet
- Pass onto the next question
- By the end of an initial pass the candidate may have answered half or a quarter of the question. But they should be confident that those answers are correct
- Make a second pass again covering subsequent questions with a blank piece of paper
- The candidate may have gathered useful information from other Examination questions
- Still be prepared not to answer questions if unsure
- Make a third pass and if necessary guess an answer
- Check the paper for completeness but do not amend any answers

Sample Paper

Below are a few questions from a sample paper. They will give the potential candidate a feel for the style of foundation questions. They also illustrate the level of detail a candidate must master.

1 *Which role, or group, has a core responsibility for providing an information hub for the programme:-*
   a) *The Programme Office*
   b) *The Programme Manager*
   c) *The Business Change Manager*
   d) *Programme Assurance*

2 *Within MSP a key element of Programme Management is to write a Blueprint. Which of the following best describes the use of this document:-*
   a) *To define the structure and composition of the work that needs to be completed in order to achieve the vision*
   b) *To maintain the programme's focus on delivering the required transformation and business change*
   c) *To enable the draft Programme Brief to be created*
   d) *To define the structure of the Programme Management Team*

3   *A Benefit Profile should include details of:-*
    a) *Dependencies, links and ownership responsibilities*
    b) *The cost of the project(s) that will deliver the output required*
    c) *The manager responsible for the project(s)*
    d) *All the above (A, B and C)*

4   *There are several different types of benefits. They are:-*
    a) *Definite, indefinite and approximate*
    b) *Financial, non-financial and intangible*
    c) *Direct financial, direct non-financial and indirect*
    d) *Tangible, intangible and financial*

5   *According to MSP, a Programme Management approach should be applied:-*
    a) *Only to those programmes where very detailed outcomes are required*
    b) *To only those programmes which are likely to be successful*
    c) *Flexibly and with different emphasis to suit the nature and the particular needs of the programme*
    d) *Only if the senior management of the organisation feel it is necessary to add additional bureaucracy to the programme*

6   *MSP states that quality, as applied to a programme, embraces many different aspects. Which one of the following is not one of those aspects:*
    a) *The quality of the programme's leadership and management processes*
    b) *The quality of the training for those employed by the programme*
    c) *The quality of its deliverables*
    d) *The quality of its assessment and measurement activities*

7   *Under Configuration Management, which role, or group, is responsible for designing the baselines appropriate to the Programme:-*
    a) *The Business Change Manager*
    b) *The Senior Responsible Owner*
    c) *The Programme Office*
    d) *The Programme Manager*

8   *Which product is an output from the process Managing the Portfolio:-*
    a) *Project lessons learned reports*
    b) *Project organisation structures*
    c) *Project progress reports*
    d) *Portfolio plans*

Sample Answers

Here are the answers to those questions with cross references to the relevant text in the MSP book. The question is repeated after each answer.

ID: 68   Manual Reference Page: 3.14   Answer: A

1   Which role, or group, has a core responsibility for providing an information hub for the programme:-
    a) The Programme Office
    b) The Programme Manager
    c) The Business Change Manager
    d) Programme Assurance

ID: 9   Manual Reference Page: App B   Answer: B

2   Within MSP a key element of Programme Management is to write a Blueprint. Which of the following best describes the use of this document:-
    a) To define the structure and composition of the work that needs to be completed in order to achieve the vision
    b) To maintain the programme's focus on delivering the required transformation and business change
    c) To enable the draft Programme Brief to be created
    d) To define the structure of the Programme Management Team

ID: 37   Manual Reference Page: 4.6   Answer: A

3   A Benefit Profile should include details of:-
    a) Dependencies, links and ownership responsibilities
    b) The cost of the project(s) that will deliver the output required
    c) The manager responsible for the project(s)
    d) All the above (A, B and C)

ID: 24   Manual Reference Page: 4.5.1   Answer: C

4   There are several different types of benefits. They are:-
    a) Definite, indefinite and approximate
    b) Financial, non-financial and intangible
    c) Direct financial, direct non-financial and indirect
    d) Tangible, intangible and financial

ID: 96   Manual Reference Page: App A   Answer: C

5   According to MSP, a Programme Management approach should be applied:-
    a) Only to those programmes where very detailed outcomes are required
    b) To only those programmes which are likely to be successful
    c) Flexibly and with different emphasis to suit the nature and the particular needs of the programme
    d) Only if the senior management of the organisation feel it is necessary to add additional bureaucracy to the programme

ID: 12   Manual Reference Page: 9.1   Answer: B

6 **MSP states that quality, as applied to a programme, embraces many different aspects. Which one of the following is not one of those aspects:**
  a) The quality of the programme's leadership and management processes
  b) The quality of the training for those employed by the programme
  c) The quality of its deliverables
  d) The quality of its assessment and measurement activities

ID: 40   Manual Reference Page: 9.2.3   Answer: D

7 **Under Configuration Management, which role, or group, is responsible for designing the baselines appropriate to the Programme:-**
  a) The Business Change Manager
  b) The Senior Responsible Owner
  c) The Programme Office
  d) The Programme Manager

ID: 93   Manual Reference Page: Tab 14.1   Answer: A

8 **Which product is an output from the process Managing the Portfolio:-**
  a) Project lessons learned reports
  b) Project organisation structures
  c) Project progress reports
  d) Portfolio plans

The Intermediate and Practitioner Examinations - Are they for you?

Many potential examination candidates wonder if they should attempt the Intermediate and Practitioner Examinations at the same time as they sit the Foundation Examination. This section may help you decide if you are ready for the Practitioner Examination or should only attempt the Intermediate Examination.

As we know programme management is the co-ordinated management of a portfolio of projects that change organisations to achieve benefits that are of strategic importance. Programme Management therefore involves:

- Working within and changing the **Culture** of an organisation
- Delivering products at an acceptable **Pace** and
- Realising **Benefits**.
- The art of programme management is to balance the impact on an organisation of using programme management tools to effect **Culture, Pace & Benefits**.

Practitioner level examiners want to be convinced that candidates understand the application of Programme Management and MSP. Candidates are expected to write freely on what they believe are the issues, and how they would tackle them within the context of MSP. Many of the questions require candidates to cross-relate different elements of MSP or to explain the importance of one particular aspect.

Examination Candidates

People come to Programme Management from various directions. Each type of candidate faces a different challenge when mastering programme management at practitioner level.

Business Managers

Business Managers may already be familiar with the culture of large organisations and how they measure benefits at a strategic level. If so, they will need to master generic project management techniques. Then they can apply their experience and knowledge in the Practitioner Examination.

If business managers are not currently operating at a strategic level, they are advised to defer the practitioner examination until a later date but should consider sitting the Intermediate Examination with the Foundation Examination.

Project Managers

Project Managers may already be familiar with project management tools such as PRINCE2. If so, they will need to master wider business topics such as strategic planning and organisational politics. Then they can apply their experience and knowledge in the Practitioner Examination.

If project managers are not currently fully conversant with a good range of project management tools i.e. operating at or above PRINCE2® practitioner level, they are also advised to defer the practitioner examination until a later date but might sit the Intermediate and the Foundation Examinations together.

Project Administrators

Project Administrators may already have observed organisational culture change, strategic planning and project management. If so they will need to formulate their own ideas on how these tools can be used effectively. Then they can apply their experience and knowledge in the Practitioner Examination.

If project administrators are not currently working across a broad spectrum of project and business support activities, they are should defer the Practitioner Examination but sit the Intermediate and Foundation Examination at the same time.

The Intermediate Examination
Prerequisites

Candidates cannot sit the Intermediate Examination until they have passed the Foundation Examination. Administratively this presents few problems and examination invigilators can informally mark foundation papers in minutes. So a candidate can plan to sit the Foundation and Intermediate Examinations on the same or subsequent days.

Examination Format

The Intermediate Examination is a closed book examination but it is not a memory test. Making the examination closed book was actually an attempt to make the examination easier not harder. If open book, examiners would have had to ask more complex questions.

With a closed book examination the questions can be quite straightforward. They are simply asking if the candidates can apply the basics of MSP. If the examiner wants the answer to be in a particular format, there will be an attachment to the examination paper which is gives the relevant structure from the MSP manual.

The examination also includes a scenario. Inevitably this scenario must be about a small programme. Indeed to make the scenario simple enough to be understood in the short time available to candidates, the scenario describes a situation that might be too small to be managed as a programme.

Preparation for the Examination

If candidates are familiar with the PRINCE2 Practitioner Examination, they should revise the technique they used for passing that examination. If not they will need to practice a wide range of practice questions. It is not the authors' intention to provide a comprehensive set of questions here. But some practice questions are included later to give the potential candidate a feel for the level of the examination.

But first here are some hints and tips on how to tackle the MSP Intermediate Examination.

Hints and Tips during the Examination

Some candidates will not have sat an examination for some time; others will be familiar with exams that have differing formats. This note is intended to assist you to hone your examination technique.

Timing

It is essential that the candidate manages their time. Candidates should recognise that it is easy to spend too much time on questions that your prefer.

There are 75 marks to be gained over one and a half hours (90 minutes) in both the Intermediate and Practitioner examinations. Allowing for overruns and for tidying up at the end, this is a mark a minute.

Every minute a candidate spends writing they should ask themselves: "Will I score a mark for that?"

The Basics

Candidates should read each question. There is time to do this before starting writing. This means more than speed-reading. The question will have been carefully constructed to be un-ambiguous and to give the candidate a vehicle for demonstrating their knowledge.

The question may be broken into parts. If it asks the candidate to consider say 2 or 5 documents then they should break the answer into halves or fifths as appropriate. Going further, if a question refers to a document that contains six parts and asks the candidate to comment on where the information would come from and who would provide it there are 6 x 2 = 12 parts.

There are unlikely to be any marks for a preamble. So candidates should not write one. If the candidate knows there are 12 parts to a question, they should cover all 12 parts.

The candidate may have strong views on certain topics. They should not lecture the marker. At intermediate level they should answer the question as put not the question they would like to answer.

The Marking Guide
The examiners have a loosely structured marking guide. There are no right or wrong answers. If a question asks you about the impact of something on 5 documents, there is not a fixed list of 5 documents that the examiner is looking for.

But the impact on some documents will be greater than on others. If the candidate chooses a document that is unrelated, they may not have much to write.
- Candidates will not get marks for generalisations.
- Candidates will not get marks for quoting the manual.
- Candidates will not get marks for stating the obvious: "Record risks in the risk log."
- The marker will be feeling generous if he gives a mark for a simple sentence. Candidates are more likely to have to write several sentences before they can gain even a single mark.
- Candidates must therefore write enough - more that a few pages per question.

Sample Scenario
This is about one third of a typical scenario:

A national retailer, Buyitall plc, has decided to review and revise the way it carries out the training of its 1,800 staff members. The company sell mainly clothing, hardware and home furnishings at low prices with a high turnover but low profit margins.

They currently run 385 stores spread throughout the UK and have a headquarters office in Sheffield. They have two main training centres, one in London and the other at the HQ in Sheffield. In Sheffield they also have accommodation for up to 50 people with 5 training suites whilst in London they have accommodation for 35 people and 3 training suites. Virtually all their staff training is currently carried out in these 2 centres with staff from all over the UK having to travel to one of these locations and then staying for the duration of the course most of which are 2/3 days long. The training covers a wide range from general management and development training through department specific training, such as shoe sizing and fitting courses, to very specific courses, such as shop window display design. All training is managed and co-ordinated by the Sheffield HQ.

The intention is to reduce the central training as much as possible by establishing smaller training facilities in ten different centres around the country. Each of these centres would have a small staff of a manager, one or more trainers, as necessary, and admin support. The staff at each centre would provide most of the training with the assistance of a group of a further 5 trainers for specific subjects who would be based in Sheffield but travel throughout the UK. A very small proportion (up to 5%) of the very specialised training will be outsourced. The training facilities at Sheffield will be retained but reduced to only 2 suites and accommodation for only 15 people. The only training carried out here will be where there is such a small demand that one national course is the only cost-effective option, or where expensive specialised equipment needs to be provided such as for the two day "Electronic-safe Management" course where a demonstration "safe" would cost £10,000.

It is envisaged there will need to be four projects within the programme.

A review of the training prospectus has shown that a significant number of the 85 courses run currently could be deleted, replaced by other training methods such as distance learning, or combined with other courses. All training material needs to be reviewed and brought up to date and this will form the basis of the "Training Design project".

The establishment of the ten new training facilities will require the lease or purchase of suitable accommodation, their refitting and equipping with IT and administrative facilities including connection to the main IT wide area network, desk chair, filing cabinets and telephone connections.

The revised working practices to allow the new system to be managed effectively in Sheffield with centralised bookings and co-ordination will need to be determined. This is the "HR project" that will also address all the relocation issues for the trainers and any other similar issues.

The "Outsourcing project" will deal with all the contractual matters associated with the outsourcing of some of the training courses. In addition, where facilities are to be leased or purchased, they will deal with all the associated legal and contractual issues.

There is will be a central programme staff based in Sheffield and each project will be run under PRINCE2 with an appropriate project team.

Sample Questions

Here then are some intermediate questions that could be set against that scenario.

Each question is worth 25 marks divided between the parts of the question (where applicable) as shown.

1 (a) Design a suitable programme management team to run this programme based on the roles described in MSP. For each role, suggest a suitable person or group for the role and give reasons for your choice. (10 marks)

1 (b) Select one of the roles you have proposed and using the check list at attachment 1 draft outline Terms of Reference for this role. (15 marks)

2 Using the Risk Register format at attachment 2 suggest three major risks to the programme. For each risk you have suggested, complete an evaluation and suggest suitable actions to take to manage the risk effectively. (25 marks)

3 One of the key benefits of the programme is allowing staff with family commitments to undertake more training to improve their chances for promotion and increase their personal development. Using the section headings at attachment 3, draft an outline benefits profile for this potential benefit. (25 marks)

4 (a) As advisor to the newly appointed Programme Manger suggest the main activities that the Programme Manager should undertake before the Shareholders' meeting in May. (10 marks)

4 (b) For each of the Directors listed in the scenario, suggest how they should be asked to provide support to the new programme. This should highlight key activities they should be expected to perform and any other help, advice, decision making, resource or other support they should be expected to provide. (15 marks)

5 (a) Attachment 4 shows two examples of a Vision Statement for the programme. Decide which is the better of the two and why. (10 marks)

5 (b) Draft a Vision Statement of your own which better meets the requirements for this programme. (15 marks)

Attachment 1
Terms of Reference
- Job Title
- Job Description
- Main Responsibilities
- Key Tasks
- Authority
  - Over other staff
  - From senior staff

Attachment 2
- Risk Register
- Unique Reference
- Risk Description
- Description of Impact
- Proximity
- Probability
- Severity
- Risk Owner
- Response
- Current Status

Attachment 3
Benefit Profile
- Description of Benefit
- Interdependencies on other benefits
- When the benefit is expected to occur and over what period will realisation take place
- Measure for the realisation of the benefit and how it will be carried out
- The "before" state measurement to include financial valuations if possible
- Key performance indicators in the business operations that will be affected by the benefit, immediately after realisation and for the future, and current or baseline performance levels.
- Details of changes that will be required to the current business processes and operations in order for the benefit to be realised
- Costs associated with realisation and measurement
- Project(s) within the programme directly related to the realisation of the benefit
- Any dependencies on risks or other programmes or projects
- Individual responsible for realisation of the benefit and who will "own" the benefit profile during the programme.

Attachment 4

Vision Statements

This programme will deliver a new flexibility for our workforce to make them appreciate how keen the senior management is to help them increase the company's profits. Within three years we will have the best trained staff of any national retail chain and will be able to forge ahead with new product lines and new ways of selling based on the leanest, keenest staff around. Profits will rise as turnover increases and we expect to see a 50% increase in sales per staff member within 5 years. The extra costs of doing training all over the country will be more than offset by the selling-off of the London estate and the reduction in the Sheffield office requirements. People will lose less time doing training which will mean will have lower recruitment requirements and this will also reduce costs.

This programme will make training much more accessible to staff and so increase training opportunities for staff and hence improve their promotion prospects. They will be able to train in a way that suits them and so take advantage of the training available with reduced opportunity costs and fewer lost productive work days.

Sample Marking Scheme

Here is a marking guide for Question 2. It highlights that the examiners have a precise structure within which the candidate can score marks. If the candidate fails to understand and answer within the marking structure, they are unlikely to score well.

	Using the Risk Register format at attachment 2 suggest three major risks to the programme. For each risk you have suggested, complete an evaluation and suggest suitable actions to take to manage the risk effectively. (25 marks)	Marks
1	Do they understand risk management?	1
2	Maximum of 8 marks per risk as long as the risk identified is programme level, not project level, with the following distribution depending on the nature of the risks selected.	24
	Description - 2 if the true nature of the risk is covered in the description	
	Impact - 2 for a comprehensive assessment of likely impact on the programme	
	Proximity - 0.5	
	Probability - 0.5	
	Severity - 0.5	
	Owner - 0.5	
	Response - 0.5 per option given to a maximum of 1.5 for a set of appropriate actions.	
	The distribution of marks can be changed if this is appropriate for a particular risk identified.	

The Practitioner Examination

Prerequisites

Candidates cannot pass the Practitioner Examination until they have passed the Intermediate Examination. However it takes a considerable length of time for Intermediate Examinations to be marked, about two months. So candidates are permitted to sit both examinations at the same time. If the candidate passes the Practitioner but fails the Intermediate, the Practitioner paper is held in abeyance until they have re-sat and passed the Intermediate Examination,

Examination Format

The Practitioner Examination is based complex scenario which, at the time of printing, is centred on a very large and complicated business process re-engineering (BPR) programme set in a national utility company. Candidates are issued with this case study some time before the examination. The examination itself is open book and candidates may take into the examination:

- Manuals such as this book and the MSP manual
- Printed Courseware, and
- Notes they have made about the case study in preparation for the examination.

Examination Preparation

We cannot over-emphasise the necessity for thorough preparation for this examination. Candidates must analyse the case study in detail and consider how programme management might operate in this culture. While some of this preparation can and must be undertaken as private study, experience has shown that it is essential for delegates to have the opportunity to discuss the case study and the different ways in which programme management might happen. Therefore we think it is essential that the examination is taken as part of a training course or after a practitioner level course.

Hints and Tips during the Examination - The Practitioner Examination - What's Different?

The MSP Practitioner Examination is based on a fairly short manual and a scenario that the candidate will have been studying for a week. This dictates the level of your answers. They must be sophisticated and add real value.

Know the Method

The candidate must be familiar with MSP, its terminology and structure. But, unlike the PRINCE2 examination, there are no marks for being able to navigate the method, nor are there marks for describing documents i.e. quoting from the manual. That detailed level of knowledge will have been tested in the Intermediate Examination.

Think Strategically

Programmes bring about strategic change. Therefore, some of those involved will be very senior, often at board level. The candidate must demonstrate that they understand what motivates senior staff and how they interact.

Use the Scenario

Programme management is about more than the structured programme environment. It is as much about the relationship between the programme environment and the external environment. In preparation for the examination candidates must think about the external environment that is described in the scenario.

Answer Tone

Candidates are unlikely to be asked to describe a document at Practitioner level – that again is an Intermediate level question. Candidates need to go into greater depth and add value. Candidates cannot just explain MSP; they must demonstrate understanding of the repercussions of MSP elements.

Therefore, you may be asked to give a critique on an example of a document. You may be asked to discuss the implications, or difficulties associated with creating a document, or to discuss the impact on the organisation as a whole or externally.

Types of Question

There are three types of question, which are summarised below. Candidates should consider how they would approach each type of question. They should try to identify what type of question is being asked.

Code	Class	Example	Amplification
I	**Interpret** the Scenario	Produce a Benefits Profile	From Scenario
C	**Context** Set by Scenario	Why is a QMS important?	Scenario is background
			Half way house
			A QMS is in MSP.
			What would it look like in this scenario?
N	**Navigate** Manual	Cross Relate Process, Document, Role	Minimal Scenario

Sample Question

The scenario is too large to include or even summarise here. But the way in which a practitioner question must be answered is clearly illustrated in the sample answers below.

Provide reasons why Benefit Profiles should be formally produced and documented, and how they would relate to the Benefit Management Strategy. (**15 marks**)

Types of Answers Expected

A "good" answer would say things like:-
- *Formalised Benefit Profiles help to avoid the misunderstandings which can arise when verbal "understandings" are used.*
- *They provide a common document which ensures that all interested parties have the same understanding of why a change is necessary, and hence why it is important that they play their part in achieving the change. As such they form a key input into the Stakeholder Management process.*

A "poor" answer would say things like:-
- *A benefit profile defines what each benefit to a programme will be, and defines a method of measuring it.*

The first answer shows that the candidate understands why "formalising" and "documenting" is important. It also shows why "producing" them is important by getting behind the mechanics of the document to identify key ways in which the information they contain important. Other aspects are just as acceptable, such as "making people think through the issues required to produce the profiles". NB If the question had asked for this "in the context of the BPR programme", it would also have been important to give illustrative examples from the scenario. The second answer is just describing the profile, not really answering the "why" bit.

22 List of definitions

Assurance
Independent assessment and confirmation that the programme as a whole or any of its aspects are on track, applying relevant practices and procedures, and that the projects, activities and business rationale remain aligned to the programme's objectives.

Audit
Objective and independent examination to ensure that the programme is being implemented effectively and according to agreement.

Baseline
A starting point or specification laid down in a document. Changes are defined with respect to the baseline. A baseline can be changed, but only following formal approval by those who approved the original baseline. The original baseline document remains available as a reference for later evaluations.

Benefit
The quantifiable and measurable improvement resulting from an outcome which is perceived as positive by a stakeholder and which will normally have a tangible value expressed in monetary or resource terms. Benefits are expected when a change is conceived. Benefits are realized as a result of activities undertaken to effect the change.

Benefits management
A continuous process running throughout the programme. The process aimed at ensuring that the maximum benefit possible within the programme are achieved. It includes identifying, optimizing, planning, monitoring and adjusting the benefits realization, and then measuring and assessing the benefits realized.

Benefits Management Strategy
How the programme will handle benefits management.

Benefits Profile
A complete description of the individual benefit (including the dis-benefits).

Benefits Realization Plan
A schedule for realizing all benefits in their mutual coherence and with assessment points.

Blueprint
A description of the future environment that management wishes to achieve in implementing the programme to deliver the capability described in the Vision Statement. This contains, amongst other things, a description of the people and their skills, working practices and processes, organizational structures, quality systems, information and reporting systems, and the necessary technical infrastructure.

Business Case

The corporate justification for the programme and projects within it, providing an answer to the question: "Why are we carrying out this programme?". It is developed by weighing up goals and benefits to be achieved against the overall costs, timeframe and the risks of the programme.

Business Case management

The process aimed at ensuring management of the Business Case during the programme. It includes the processes of setting-up an initial Business Case and assessing and updating the Business Case during the programme. It ensures that the programme's rationale, objectives, benefits and risks are balanced favourably against the financial investment and that this balance is maintained, adjusted and assessed throughout the programme.

Business Change Manager

Person responsible for Benefits Management, normally appointed for each of the business units affected by the programme. They are responsible from identification of the benefits through to the embedding of the new capability delivered by the projects in order to realize the benefits whilst maintaining appropriate business as usual activities.

Capability

A service, function or process which the organization can exploit to realize benefits.

Change

The alteration of a situation from the current to a new state.

Change Control

Controlling changes in specification with regard to a baseline.

Communication management

The process aimed at making communication with the stakeholders as effective as possible. Communication management involves planning, monitoring and managing communication with the stakeholders. Measuring the effectiveness of the communication and managing effectively the feedback from stakeholders are also important aspects. Communication management is a part of stakeholder management.

Communications Manager

The person responsible for communication management, an optional role in support of the Programme Manager.

Communication Plan

The plan describing who communicates what information, when, how, to whom and how these activities are managed during the programme.

Configuration Manager

The person responsible for configuration management, a role normally carried out by the Programme Office.

Configuration management

The process aimed at managing the configuration, including configuration identification, configuration change control, configuration status responsibility and configuration audit.

Design authority / architect

The person responsible for the internal and external consistency of the Blueprint. Internal consistency covers the mutual connection of the processes, organization, technology and information of the new organization. External consistency covers the connection between the Blueprint and the programme's end goal that is to be realized. This is an optional role supporting the Programme Manager.

Dis-benefit

An unwanted outcome of a change. A negative quantification of an outcome.

Earned Value Analysis

A method of measuring the progress of a project or programme based on the budgeted costs of work already carried out.

Enabler

Project or activity with the goal of delivering an envisaged outcome but that which of itself may not deliver any specific benefit.

End goal

The unique strategic goal to be achieved with the programme.

Financial Manager

The person responsible for setting-up and managing the financial plan, as well as managing the programme expenses. It is an optional role in support of the Programme Manager.

Gateway review

A formal evaluation on a point of decision-making (go/no go) in order to ensure the programme is effective and is likely to deliver what has been agreed.

Governance (as used in MSP)

All the functions, responsibilities, processes and procedures that define how the programme is set-up, managed and controlled.

Highlight Report

A periodic report describing the main points of the project's progress.

Issue

A problem, query, concern or request for change affecting the programme and requiring the consideration of management to be solved or dealt with.

Issue Log

A document containing all issues arising during the programme. The Issue Log includes the description of all issues, the decisions taken and the current status.

Issue resolution
The process that ensures that issues are managed effectively. It includes collecting, registering and analysing issues, taking decisions and initiatives, and monitoring agreed actions.

Issue Resolution Strategy
The approach to the process for managing issues.

Key Performance Indicator (KPI)
An important characteristic of an operation, service or function in a particular environment, based on which performance is measured. It is the standard against which something is measured or a goal realized.

Mission
The legitimacy of the organization's existence.

Multi-organization programme
A programme implemented by two or more organizations with a joint end goal.

Multi-project management
The management of a group of (existing and future) projects with no mutual connection other than the fact that these projects use the same staff and resources.

Net present value
A methodology whereby flows of money quantified at various points are rendered comparable with one another by calculating the current value of these money flows.

Objective
The value to be achieved as referring to a (unique) performance indicator.

Outcome
A product or service brought about by an enabler. The effect of a change the measurement of which is a benefit.

Output
The end result of a project or activity, itself delivering no direct benefit since only the embedding of the new capability delivered as a result of the output can deliver benefits.

Peer review
An internal independent review by colleagues from the same or related organization that can be carried out at any time during the programme.

Performance
A condition of a quality of an object in a specified environment.

Portfolio management
The co-ordination of a number of projects that together produce new capabilities necessary for delivering one or more joint goals.

Post-programme review

One or more evaluations carried out after the programme has been closed to determine whether the expected benefits of the programme, as envisaged by the SRO, have been realized.

Post-project review

One or more evaluations carried out after the project has been carried out to determine whether the goal delivered by the project result, as envisaged by the Project Executive, has been or is being realized.

Product

Input or output of a project or activity that can be described in a tangible and/or quantitative manner.

Programme

A portfolio of connected projects and activities that are co-ordinated and managed as a unit such that they achieve one or more strategically important pre-defined objectives and realize benefits.

Programme assurance

Ensuring that the programme is effective and will deliver what has been agreed. Responsibility for this lies with the individual members of the Sponsoring Group, as well as the Senior Responsible Owner and the Programme Manager.

Programme Board

The management platform complementing the role of Senior Responsible Owner, mainly used for programmes where a single individual does not have sufficient 'power' within his own organization for carrying out the role of Senior Responsible Owner.

Programme Brief

A description of the main points of the programme, including the initial description of the objectives, desired benefits, risks, costs and timeframe of the programme.

Programme Definition

The collection of information that defines what must be achieved with the programme and how this will be realized. The Programme Definition includes the Vision Statement, the Blueprint, the Business Case, the organizational structure, the Project Portfolio, the Benefits Profiles, and the Stakeholder Map.

Programme Director

A title previously used in the MSP method for the role of Senior Responsible Owner.

Programme management

The co-ordinated organization, management and implementation of a series of connected projects and activities for realizing one or more strategically important pre-defined objectives.

Programme Management Team

A term used to indicate the total management of a programme, including the Sponsoring

Group, Senior Responsible Owner, the Programme Manager, the Business Change Managers, the Programme Office and any support roles such as the Financial Manager, Communications Manager and members of the Programme Board.

Programme Manager
The person responsible for the set-up, management and delivery of the programme. Typically allocated to a single individual.

Programme Mandate
The trigger to start a programme from the senior management who are sponsoring the programme. Preferably this should be a document defining the main points of the programme, and placing these within the framework of the business mission, objectives, strategies and other initiatives. It is the reason for starting the 'Identifying a programme' process.

Programme Office
This is the organizational unit providing technical and administrative support to the programme. The Programme Office is particularly responsible for collecting and issuing the necessary information and reports. It can also offer support to the projects within the programme.

Programme organization
The organization of the programme with a description of the tasks, responsibilities and authority of the individual roles and the allocation of these roles to specific persons.

Programme Plan
A comprehensive document scheduling the projects, their costs, resources, risks, and transition activities together with monitoring and control activities.

Programme review
An evaluation to see whether the pre-set objectives have or are being achieved. This evaluation can also be used to analyse the successes and mistakes in the programme management process. An evaluation carried out at the end of the programme is referred to as a post-programme review.

Project
A series of connected activities within a temporary organization for delivering a pre-defined outcome under set conditions within time, quality, resource and cost constraints.

Project Board
The management platform where senior management from the client and the supplier come together in a project for decision-making and providing commitment for all issues regarding the project.

Project Brief
A description of the main points of a project and the basis for the authorization for starting the "Initiating a project" process.

Project dependency network

A summary of the inputs and results of various projects and how they contribute to or depend on other projects.

Project Executive

Represents programme management within the project and is ultimately responsible for the project to programme management. He is also the Chair of the Project Board and responsible for ensuring the project is realized within the project Business Case.

Project initiation document (PID)

Document containing a collection of details necessary for starting a project properly, the basis for approving the budget and for the authorization of implementing the project.

Project management

A co-ordinated organization and management of a series of connected activities for delivering a pre-defined output, deliverable or product.

Project Manager

The person responsible for the daily management of the project.

Project plan

Overall plan showing the most important products, delivery dates and production costs of a project together with the necessary resources and dependencies.

Project Portfolio

The collection of projects and activities within a programme, the total of which should together deliver the capabilities as described in the Blueprint.

Project result

The tangible or intangible product, deliverable or output of a project used by the programme to achieve the programme's end goal.

Quality management

The process aimed at ensuring the client's expectations are satisfied.

Quality Management Strategy

How the programme will achieve the required levels of quality in the way that the programme is managed and directed, and how the programme's deliverables will be assessed for "fitness for purpose".

Quality Review

A formal evaluation to establish whether what has been delivered satisfies the demands set ('fit for purpose' and 'fit for use').

Resource Management Strategy

Description of the necessary staff and resources during the programme and how these resources are managed effectively.

Risk

A negative threat or positive outcome that is uncertain and that might affect the course of the programme.

Risk management

The process aimed at ensuring that risks are managed effectively.

Risk Management Strategy

The approach to effective risk management.

Risk Register

A document containing a description of all risks that might occur, or might have occurred, during the programme, and describing the potential impacts and measures taken to manage the risks.

Role

A specific range of tasks, responsibilities and accountabilities that can be allocated to one or more individuals and which can be combined or divided up in special circumstances.

Scrutiny

A formal examination by external parties to establish whether a programme is being carried out effectively and is likely to deliver what has been agreed.

Senior Responsible Owner

Represents senior management of the business organization within the programme and is ultimately responsible to the Sponsoring Group for the success of the programme, that is, the successful achievement of the desired outcomes and the realization of the expected benefits from the programme.

Sponsoring Group

Group of senior managers responsible for business units affected by the programme and responsible for the investment decision and top-level endorsement of the rational and objectives for the programme.

Stakeholder

Any individual, group or organization with an interest in or affected by the final result and/or with influence over realizing the end result.

Stakeholder management

Process aimed at ensuring the stakeholders are involved as effectively as possible in the programme. This includes identifying and analysing the stakeholders, and planning, monitoring and adjusting communications to and from the stakeholders.

Stakeholder Management Strategy

The approach to how the stakeholders are managed effectively by the programme.

Stakeholder Map

A schematic diagram in the form of a matrix showing the various stakeholders and their particular interests in the programme.

Tranche

A group of projects within the programme that delivers (part of) a new capability or capabilities for the business organization and is used to make the programme easier to manage.

Transition

Implementation and embedding the new or changed capabilities into the business organization so that they become business as usual and realize the expected benefits.

Vision

A description prepared from the business's perspective as to what the programme must deliver.

Vision Statement

An outward facing description of the new capabilities resulting from the programme's delivery.

23 Organization of management products

23.1 Benefits Management Strategy

Purpose
Clearly establishing how benefits are to be managed effectively.

The Benefits Management Strategy describes the benefits of the programme, the mutual dependencies between the benefits, and the responsibilities involved in identifying, defining, realizing and measuring the benefits.

Description
Describing the benefits
- The main points of all the benefits
- In which business units the benefits must be realized.

Benefits model
- Model of benefits including interdependencies
- Dependencies on specific areas of change required within the business.

Responsibilities for realizing the benefits
- Functions and roles with responsibility for planning and realizing benefits (aligned with the programme organization)
- Individuals responsible for the respective functions and roles.

Benefits evaluation process
- How, when and by whom the benefits are to be evaluated.

Responsibilities
- The Programme Manager is responsible for preparing and implementing the Benefits Management Strategy
- The Business Change Manager supports the Programme Manager in preparing and implementing the strategy
- The Senior Responsible Owner owns and must approve the strategy.

Derived from
- Vision Statement
- Blueprint.

Context
- Is prepared during the DP process
- Provides input for the Benefits Realization Plan and the Programme Plan
- Is input for the GP process for setting-up and managing the programme
- Defines the Benefits Management process carried out in the MB process
- Is evaluated during the tranche reviews (GP) and the CP process.

23.2 Benefit Profile

Purpose
Creating a basis for focusing the attention of all parties concerned on the benefits to be realized.

A Benefits profile includes a detailed description of the benefit and dis-benefit. It states which capabilities must be realized to make the benefits possible, when the benefits are realized, who is responsible for realizing the benefits and how they must be measured.

Description
Description of the benefit (or dis-benefit)
- Detailed description of the benefit
- Why this benefit is necessary.

Dependencies regarding other benefits
- The dependency of the benefits on other benefits, if applicable.

Planning
- From which moment or milestone can the benefit be realized
- Over what period must the benefit be realized.

Performance values regarding the benefit
- Performance values regarding the benefit:
  - The baseline measurement
  - Various values in the period during which the benefit is developed during the programme
  - The final values of the KPIs to be achieved
- How the performance values are to be measured, by whom and when
- The financial value of the benefit.

KPIs operational management
- Which Key Performance Indicators (KPIs) in operational management are influenced by the realization of the benefit and for each KPI:
  - The baseline measurement
  - Various values in the period during which the benefit is developed during the programme
  - The final values of the KPIs to be achieved.

Related changes in operational management
- Which changes in operational management are necessary to achieve the change.

Costs
- What extra costs must be incurred in the operation in order to realize the benefit
- What costs must be incurred in order to be able to measure the benefit.

Related projects
- Which projects deliver the capabilities necessary for realizing the benefit.

Dependencies
- Risks affecting realization of the benefit
- Dependencies on other projects and programmes.

Responsibilities
- The business units within which the benefit will be realized
- The Business Change Manager is the owner of the Benefits Profiles and is responsible for preparing and updating these.

Derived from
- Vision Statement
- Blueprint.

Context
- Is prepared during the DP process
- Is part of the Programme Definition
- Delivers input for the Benefits Realization Plan, the Project Portfolio, the Programme Plan, the

Business Case and the Risk Register
- Is input for the GP process for setting-up and managing the programme
- Is refined during the MP process when setting and adapting the scope of the projects
- Is input for the MB process and is updated during this process
- Is evaluated during the tranche reviews (GP) and the CP process.

23.3 Benefits Realization Plan

Purpose
Providing a basis for realizing the benefits and for monitoring their implementation.

The Benefits Realization Plan includes the timing, stating when and which extra transition activities must be carried out in order to implement the project results into the respective business organizations, when the various benefits must be realized, and when the various benefits reviews must be held.

Description
Timing
- Plan stating when benefits or groups of benefits must actually be realized
  - Starting date and starting value of benefits realization
  - Planned realization over time
  - Final value for benefits realization at the end of the programme
  - Forecasted final value (after the programme).

Milestones
- Checks at which the benefits are measured and evaluated.

Transition activities
- Transition activities within the programme aimed at the business organization to ensure the benefits realization, measuring and monitoring activities are continued after the programme has been closed.

Responsibilities
- The Programme Manager is the owner of the Benefits Realization Plan and is responsible for its preparation, monitoring and updating
- The Senior Responsible Owner provides input and finally approves the plan.

It is important for the Benefits Realization Plan to be prepared in close co-operation with the owners of the various benefits to be realized and the Business Change Managers.

Derived from
- Benefits Profiles
- Benefits Management Strategy
- Programme Plan.

Context
- Is prepared during the DP process
- Delivers input for the Programme Plan (and vice versa) and for the Risk Register
- Is the basis for monitoring the progress of benefits realization during the programme in the GP process
- Is updated in the MP process following progress of the projects
- Is the basis for implementation and monitoring of benefits realization by the Business Change

Managers in the MB process and is refined and updated in this process
- Is evaluated during the tranche reviews (GP) and the CP process.

It can be convenient to combine the Programme Plan and the Benefits Realization Plan. However, one must beware of a reduction in senior management attention to the benefits to be realized if both plans are combined.

23.4 Blueprint

Purpose
Providing a basis for focusing the attention of all parties concerned on what must be achieved in order to realize the desired end goal and the expected benefits.

The Blueprint describes the new or improved capabilities of the business organization. It may include the intermediate stages (at the end of the tranches) while implementing the programme, necessary to realize the benefits of the programme.

Description
Processes
- Describing the new and/or changed business processes and operations
- Describing the associated planning, management and facilitating processes required in the future state.

Organization
- Describing the new organization structure with the roles and associated tasks, responsibilities and authorities necessary to support the future business operations
- Describing new staff skills
- Describing changes in culture and attitude necessary for achieving the desired end goal and realizing the desired benefits.

Technology
- Describing the new and/or improved technology necessary for implementing the new capabilities such as ICT systems, buildings, machines, vehicles and equipment.

Information
- Describing the data and information necessary for future business operations
- Describing the necessary changes or redevelopment of information and data for the future state.

These include the Key Performance Indicators regarding the performance levels, service levels and operational costs of the respective departments.

Responsibilities
- The Programme Manager is responsible for preparing, monitoring and updating the Blueprint
- The Senior Responsible Owner is owner of the Blueprint
- The Sponsoring Group must approve the Blueprint.

Derived from
- Programme Mandate
- Programme Brief
- Vision Statement.

Context

- Is prepared during the DP process
- Is part of Programme Definition
- Is prepared following and in connection with the Vision Statement and the Benefits Profiles
- Is input for the GP process for setting-up and managing the programme
- Is updated during the MP process based on the project results delivered/to be delivered
- Is input for the MB process and is updated during this process
- Is evaluated during the tranche reviews (GP) and the CP process.

23.5 Business Case

Purpose
Establishing the ongoing viability of the programme.

The Business Case includes the corporate justification for the use of resources necessary to enable the programme to succeed. The Business Case describes the comparison between the goals to be achieved, costs, timing, benefits and risks of the programme and how the programme will contribute to the overall business strategy.

The Business Case is a collection of information from other programme and project documents.

Description
Background
- Context and short history of the business/departments involved
- Analysis of the business environment
- Reason for starting the programme.

Programme goals
- The strategic goals of the programme as laid down in the Vision Statement
- Connection between programme goals on the one hand, and business strategies and business goals in the context of the internal and external business environment on the other hand.

Options
- Options considered
- The most important reasons why these options were not selected.

Benefits and results
- The expected benefits and results that the programme will deliver, considering the recognition of the organization's capability to implement the necessary changes.

Risks and issues
- The most important risks regarding the programme
- The major issues and assumptions that are important in the context of the Business Case.

A detailed summary of the risks is included in the Risk Register.

Costs and planning
- Overall estimate of the total costs of the programme
- Estimate of the timescale of the programme.

A detailed estimate of costs and time is part of the Programme Plan.

Investment appraisal
- A financial appraisal of the expected benefits versus the costs and risks connected with implementing the programme.

It is possible to set-up a cost-benefit analysis for certain programmes, or a scenario analysis based on a multi-criteria appraisal may sometimes be used.

Responsibilities
- The Programme Manager is responsible for preparing, monitoring and updating the Business Case
- The Senior Responsible Owner is the owner of the Business Case
- The Sponsoring Group must approve the Business Case.

Derived from
- Programme Brief
- Vision Statement
- Blueprint
- Programme Plan
- Benefits Profiles.

Context
- Is prepared during the DP process
- Is part of Programme Definition
- Is developed in parallel with the Blueprint to ensure the benefits to be realized form the basis for the change to be achieved by the programme
- Delivers input for the Programme Plan (and vice versa) and for the Risk Register
- Is input for the GP process for setting-up and managing the programme
- Is updated in the MP process and assessed following progress of the projects
- Is input for the MB process and is updated and assessed during this process
- Is evaluated during the tranche reviews (GP) and the CP process.

23.6 Resource Management Strategy

Purpose

Determining staff and resources needed to realize the programme, to state how these staff and resources are to be deployed, and how this effort must be managed.

The Resource Management Strategy describes the financing, the costs and the expense pattern of the programme, including the staff and resources needed and to be deployed, the HR services needed and to be deployed, and the facilities for the programme.

Description

Budget and budget monitoring
- Estimating costs and expenses in the programme, including the budget needed for managing the programme
- Costs and cash-flow planning of the programme
- Approval and procurement procedure for expenditure and expenses
- Financial reports required.

Financing
- Necessary financing, if necessary including the relevant timescales
- Procedures for financial administration and budget allocation
- Sources of finance.

Necessary facilities, infrastructure and services
- Facilities such as buildings, equipment, office space and so on
- Infrastructure such as ICT and information provision
- Supporting services.

State the use against time if appropriate and possible. Also state the necessary qualities and how these requirements will be fulfilled (sources). Finally, state the procedu-res for acquisition, maintenance, termination and possible disposal of facilities, infrastructure and services.

Deployment of staff and personnel during the transition
- Necessary deployment of staff and personnel during the transition
- HR staff required for the supervision and support of staff and personnel during the transition.

Deployment of staff and personnel Project Portfolio
- Necessary deployment of staff and personnel for the projects and activities within the Project Portfolio, sub-divided per project and spread out over time.

Also state the necessary qualities of staff and personnel, how this requirement will be fulfilled (sources), and the procedures for acquisition, training, induction, results, performance assessment and any dismissals.

Responsibilities

- The Programme Manager is responsible for preparing and implementing the Resource Management Strategy

- The Programme Management Team supports the Programme Manager in preparing and implementing the strategy
- The Senior Responsible Owner is the owner of and must approve the strategy.

Derived from
- Programme Plan.

Context
- Is prepared during the DP process
- Is part of governing the programme
- Is input for the GP process for setting-up and managing the programme
- Defines the process of deploying staff and resources in the MP and MB processes
- Is evaluated during the tranche reviews (GP) and the CP process.

23.7 Communication Plan

Purpose
Providing a basis for carrying out communication and information activities within the programme, and enabling the monitoring and assessing of the implementation of these activities.

The Communication Plan describes what is communicated when, by whom, to whom, how and by which medium.

Description
Communication objectives
- What are the communication objectives, such as:
  - Maintaining an understanding of the need for the programme
  - Ensuring that everyone knows what must be achieved
  - Creating commitment among staff and management
  - Providing clarity over and creating understanding for the changes to be implemented
  - Maximizing benefits.

Target groups
- What are the different communication target groups:
  - Within the programme
  - Within the respective departments
  - External target groups, such as customers, suppliers and government.

Communicating the content
- Which messages must be communicated, such as:
  - Why the programme is necessary
  - What must be achieved
  - Projects to be implemented and (transition) activities
  - The effect of the changes for specific target groups
  - The progress of the programme
  - Commitment from senior management
- How much information is released and to what level of detail.

Responsibilities
- Who is responsible for which elements of the communications to which specific target groups
- Which procedures apply in setting-up, approving and distributing the information.

Communication channels
- Which channels of communication will be used for which target groups and for which messages.

Communication for each target group
- Description of the communication process for each target group: what is communicated when, by whom and how.

Timing
- A bar chart with a summary of what is communicated when, by whom, how and to whom (including feedback)
- Possibly including preparation work and necessary decision-making for the communications.

Deployment of staff and resources
- How many staff and resources are required
- Which specific people must make a specific contribution at which times.

Responsibilities
- The Programme Manager is the owner of/responsible for preparing, monitoring and updating the Communication Plan
- The Senior Responsible Owner delivers input and ultimately approves the Communication Plan.

Derived from
- Stakeholder Management Strategy
- Stakeholder Map
- Vision Statement
- Blueprint.

Context
- Is prepared during the DP process
- Is the basis for implementing and monitoring communication activities in the GP, MP and MB processes and is refined and updated in these processes
- Is evaluated during the tranche reviews (GP) and the CP process.

23.8 Issue Log

Purpose
Capturing the programme issues in a clear and centralized manner in order to optimally manage these issues.

The programme issues, the possible consequences of these issues, the measures to be taken and the person responsible for this are registered in the Issue Log.

Description
- Unique Reference number
- Date of registration
- Submitted by
- Description of the issue
- Status of the issue (for example: in process, under review, measures being implemented, completed)
- Impact analysis
- Classification of seriousness of the impact of the issue on the programme
- Corrective measures (including timing and estimation of costs)
- Individuals responsible for implementing and monitoring the corrective measures and monitoring the issue
- Authorization (name and signature of authorized person)
- Status of the implementation of the measures
- Has the person submitting the issue received feedback (possibly several times, depending on the status of the issue).

Responsibilities
- The Programme Manager is responsible for issue resolution and having the Issue Log completed and updated
- The Programme Office is responsible for registering the issues in the Issue Log, and updating the Issue Log following agreement and items flowing from issue resolution.

Derived from
- Issues occurring during the programme.

Context
- Is prepared during the DP process (it is sometimes appropriate to set-up the Issue Log during the IP process)
- Is updated as part of the issue resolution in the GP, MP and MB processes
- Is evaluated during the tranche reviews (GP) and the CP process.

23.9 Issue Resolution Strategy

Purpose
Clearly establishing how issues are managed within the programme.

The Issue Resolution Strategy describes the procedures and the responsibilities for regis-tration, analysis and decision-making with regard to issues and the implementation of the measures to be taken.

Description
Issue resolution procedure
- How issues are registered and by whom
- How people can report issues
- How the impact of issues is assessed and by whom
- How corrective measures are determined and by whom
- Who takes the decisions regarding the issues
- How the implementation of the corrective actions is monitored
- How the stakeholders are involved in implementing the issues and actions resulting from this
- How the effectiveness of the measures and the solution of the issues are monitored
- How, by whom and how often communication is carried out regarding the issues, with the person submitting the issue and any other stakeholders.

Harmonizing projects
- How is the issue resolution procedure for the projects set-up
- How is the issue resolution procedure of the projects geared to the programme.

Responsibilities
- The Programme Manager is responsible for setting-up and implementing the Issue Resolution Strategy
- The Programme Management Team supports the Programme Manager in setting-up and implementing the strategy
- The Senior Responsible Owner is the owner of and must approve the strategy.

Derived from
- Previous projects and programmes
- Stakeholder Management Strategy
- Risk Management Strategy.

Context
- Is prepared during the DP process
- Is part of governing the programme
- Is input for the GP process for setting-up and governing the programme
- Defines the issue resolution in the MP and MB processes
- Is evaluated during the tranche reviews (GP) and the CP process.

23.10 Quality Management Strategy

Purpose
Clearly establishing how quality must be managed within the programme.

The Quality Management Strategy describes which quality demands and quality systems apply within the programme, how the quality assurance is regulated, and which quality controls are implemented.

Description
Quality management system
- Scope of processes, documents and results forming part of the quality management system to be applied
- The quality management system to be applied
- Company and system standards to be complied with.

Quality demands
- Most important quality criteria for programme results
- Company and product standards to be complied with.

Quality assurance, quality audit and quality control activities
- Who is responsible for these activities
- What initiates these activities (intervals, milestones and possible risks and issues occurring)
- What actions will be undertaken depending on the results of these activities.

Configuration Management and Change Control
- Configuration Management procedures and the assignment of the Configuration Manager
- Change Control procedures and the assignment of the authority to change, and any change budget.

Responsibilities
- Roles, names and functions of the people with responsibilities in the context of quality management activities
- Tasks, responsibilities and authority under the various roles for the quality management activities.

Providing the necessary information
- Information needed in order to carry out the quality management activities adequately.

Staff and resources required
- Staff required in order to carry out quality management activities.

Support tools required
- Support tools and the associated protocols for support for the quality management activities to be carried out.

Responsibilities
- The Programme Manager is responsible for preparing and implementing the Quality Management Strategy
- The Programme Management Team supports the Programme Manager in preparing and carrying out the strategy
- The Senior Responsible Owner is owner of and must approve the strategy.

Derived from
- Business quality systems
- Industrial standards
- Programme Definition.

Context
- Is prepared during the DP process
- Is part of governing the programme
- Is input for the GP process for setting-up and governing the programme
- Defines the quality management in the MP process
- Is evaluated during the tranche reviews (GP) and the CP process.

23.11 Programme Mandate

Purpose
Providing an insight into what the programme contains in order to start the 'Identifying a programme' process and to appoint a Senior Responsible Owner.

The Programme Mandate describes the desired outcome of the programme based on the business strategy and the business policy.

Description
End goal
- The end goal or goals that the organization(s) wish to achieve with the programme.

Outcomes
- What the programme delivers in terms of new services and/or new operational capabilities.

Expected benefits
- How the respective organization(s) will perform better as a result of the new services and/or operational capabilities.

Fitting in with the business strategy
- How the programme fits in with strategies of the respective organization(s).

Responsibilities
- The Programme Mandate is prepared under the responsibility of the Sponsoring Group.

Derived from
- Business strategy and / or policy.

Context
- Is input for the IP process
- Delivers input for the Programme Brief in the IP process and for the Vision Statement and the Blueprint in the DP process.

23.12 Programme organization

Purpose
Establishing the tasks, responsibilities and authorities of persons involved in managing the programme to enable clear and optimal management.

Programme organization describes the Programme organization structure, the roles within this structure, the people responsible for the various roles, the interfaces with the respective projects and business organizations, and the various meeting structures.

Description
Organization chart
- Organization chart showing the individual roles
- Allocating roles to individuals and functions.

Terms of reference
- The individual tasks, responsibilities and authorities for each role
- Which other people/roles report to the respective role
- To which other people/roles the respective role reports
- With which other people/roles the respective role must consult
- Interfaces with the roles in the respective projects
- Possibly a task responsibility matrix.

Meeting structures
- Participants in the meeting
- Roles in the meetings (Chairman, Secretary, etc.)
- Subjects/agenda/frequency of meetings
- Function/authority of meetings.

Responsibilities
- The Programme Manager is responsible for preparing, monitoring and updating the Programme organizations
- The Senior Responsible Owner is owner of the Programme organization
- The Sponsoring Group must approve the Programme organization.

Derived from
- Business organization structures
- Vision Statement
- Blueprint
- Benefits Profiles
- Project Portfolio.

Context
- Is prepared during the DP process
- Is part of the Programme Definition
- Is input for the GP process for setting-up and managing the programme

- Provides a framework for the GP, MP and MB processes
- Is evaluated during the tranche reviews (GP) and the CP process.

23.13 Programme Plan

Purpose
Providing a basis for implementing the programme and for monitoring the progress of the programme.

The Programme Plan describes the main points of the plan for implementing the programme including the transition and management activities.

Description
Project information
- The Project Portfolio including:
  - An estimate of costs and time
  - The necessary capacities
  - The relation with the benefits to be realized
- The projects dependency network.

Risks and assumptions
- The most important risks regarding the programme and the most important risk management measures
- The most important assumptions regarding the implementation of the programme.

The Risk Register includes a detailed summary of the risks and established contingency plans.

Timing
- A bar chart with the planning of the individual projects
- The grouping of projects into tranches
- The timing of reviews at the end of the individual tranches
- The timing of the most important communications within the programme
- The most important risk management measures
- The most important audits and quality controls to be implemented.

Transition plan(s)
- Delivery of data from the project outputs to the respective departments
- The transition activities for embedding the new capabilities in the normal operational management within the respective departments
- The capacities required for this.

Control activities
- Assurance and assessment activities
- Information required for review and reporting
- Performance levels to be achieved
- Responsibilities for review and reporting.

Use of staff and resources (including costs)
- The estimated deployment of staff and resources for implementing the programme.

Responsibilities
- The Programme Manager is owner of the Programme Plan and responsible for preparing, monitoring and updating it
- The Senior Responsible Owner delivers input and finally approves the Programme Plan.

Derived from
- Blueprint
- Benefits management strategy
- Benefits Profiles
- Benefits realization plan (and vice versa)
- Business Case (and vice versa)
- Project Portfolio.

Context
- Is prepared during the DP process
- Delivers input for the Benefits Realization Plan (and vice versa), the Business Case (and vice versa), the Risk Register and Resource Management Strategy
- Is the basis for monitoring the progress of the programme in total in the GP process
- Is the basis for implementing and monitoring the projects and activities in the MP and MB processes and is updated in these processes
- Is evaluated during the tranche reviews (GP) and the CP process.

23.14 Programme Brief

Purpose
Providing the Sponsoring Group with a formal basis for assessing whether the programme is sufficiently viable to start the process of Defining the programme. The Programme Brief is also the basis for preparing the Programme Definition.

The Programme Brief describes the programme goals and the main points of the programme outcome, including the recognized issues, the risks and the expected costs.

Description
Background
- Describes the changes to be implemented for realizing the business strategies and the programme goals.

Main points for the Outline Vision Statement
- A description of the ultimate goal the respective organizations wish to achieve with the programme, supported by a description of the new or improved capabilities which will be expanded to produce the final Vision Statement.

Expected benefits
- Expected benefits of the new capabilities, with an indication of the timescale over which these can be realized. Also states how these benefits can be measured.
- Also for any dis-benefits.

Risks and issues
- Risks and issues that could affect the success of the programme
- Pre-conditions, assumptions and possible conflicts that could affect the programme.

Estimates
- Estimation of costs, time and necessary use of staff and resources for establishing, managing and implementing the programme
- Initial list of projects and activities and their time estimates.

Responsibilities
- The Senior Responsible Owner is responsible for preparing the Programme Brief
- The Sponsoring Group must approve the outline Vision Statement.

Derived from
- Business strategy and policy
- Programme Mandate
- Information from the Sponsoring Group
- Information from other internal and external parties involved in the programme.

Context
- Is prepared and updated during the IP process

- Delivers input for the Vision Statement, the Blueprint and the Business Case
- Delivers input for the Sponsoring Group to enable it to assess the viability of the programme and authorize the start of the DP process.

23.15 Project Portfolio

Purpose
Providing a summary of the total of projects and activities that together will produce the final situation as described in the Blueprint.

The Project Portfolio describes the most important activities and results of the individual projects, including timing and costs of these projects, the dependencies between these projects, and the way the results of these projects contribute to the individual benefits.

Description
Summary of projects
- Description of all projects and activities within the portfolio:
  - Existing projects and activities becoming part of the programme
  - New projects and activities still to be initiated.

Project information
- Project information on the main points of the individual projects:
  - Results to be delivered
  - Timing
  - Necessary capacities
  - Relations with other projects
  - Contribution to the benefits.

Relation between projects and benefits to be realized
- Description of how the projects and activities within the portfolio contribute to the desired end goal of the programme:
  - Which projects together will deliver which capabilities
  - Which benefits must be realized with the specific capabilities.

Responsibilities
- The Programme Manager is responsible for preparing and updating the Project Portfolio.

Derived from
- Blueprint
- Benefits Profiles.

Context
- Is prepared during the DP process
- Is part of the Programme Definition
- Is used as a basis to develop the Programme Plan and also delivers input to the Risk Register
- Is input for the GP, MP and MB processes and is reviewed during these processes
- Is evaluated during the tranche reviews (GP) and the CP process.

23.16 Risk Register

Purpose
Establishing the risks of the programme in a clear and centralized manner with the goal of optimally managing these risks.

The programme risks and how these are managed is entered into the Risk Register.

Description
- Unique Reference number
- Risk category
- Description of risk
- Related projects likely to have an impact on the risk
- Impact of risk on the programme
- Probability of the risk occurring
- Classification of the severity of the impact of the risk
- Time horizon of the risk (to be defined in steps in which decision-making consultation on the risks also takes place)
- Risk profile: chance multiplied by impact
- Risk owner (name and signature of the person who must keep his finger on the pulse regarding risk)
- Agreed risk measures, including planning and cost estimates
- Persons responsible for implementing and monitoring the agreed risk measures
- Status of the implementation of the risk measures
- Status of the risk/how the risk is developing.

Responsibilities
- The Programme Manager is responsible for managing the risks and having the Risk Register completed and updated
- The Programme Office is responsible for registering the risks in the Risk Register, and updating the Register following agreements and issues flowing from the management of risks.

Derived from
- Blueprint
- Benefits Profiles
- Benefits Realization Plan
- Business Case
- Project Portfolio
- Programme Plan.

Context
- Is prepared during the DP process (it is sometimes appropriate to establish the Risk Register during the IP process)
- Is updated as part of risk management in the GP, MP and MB processes
- Is evaluated during the tranche reviews (GP) and the CP process.

23.17 Risk Management Strategy

Purpose
Clearly establishing how the risks within the programme must be managed.

The Risk Management Strategy describes the procedures and the responsibilities for risk analysis and risk management, and how the effectiveness of this is to be assured.

Description
Risk management procedure
- How and by whom are risks registered
- How can people raise risks
- How and by whom are the impacts and the probability of risks assessed
- How and by whom are the risk owners of the individual risks determined
- How and by whom are corrective measures determined
- Who takes the decisions regarding the risks (who decides, for example, the accepted tolerance levels of the risks)
- How is the implementation of corrective actions monitored
- How are stakeholders involved with risks, and in actions resulting from these
- How is the effectiveness of the measures/the management of the risks monitored
- How, by whom, how often and to which stakeholder will (the development of) the risks be communicated.

Harmonizing projects
- How is the risk management procedure of the projects set up
- How are the risk management procedures for the projects geared to that of the programme.

Responsibilities
- The Programme Manager is responsible for preparing and implementing the Risk Management Strategy
- The Programme Management Team supports the Programme Manager in preparing and implementing the strategy
- The Senior Responsible Owner is the owner of and must approve the strategy.

Derived from
- Business Risk Management Strategy
- Previous projects and programmes.

Context
- Is prepared during the DP process
- Is part of Governing a programme
- Delivers input for the Issue Resolution Strategy
- Is input for the GP processes for setting-up and managing the programme
- Defines the risk management in the MP an MB processes
- Is evaluated during the tranche reviews (GP) and the CP process.

23.18 Stakeholder Management Strategy

Purpose
Clearly establishing how relations with the stakeholders in the programme should be managed.

The Stakeholder Management Strategy describes the procedures and responsibilities for stakeholder management and how the effectiveness of this is to be assured.

Description
Stakeholder analysis
- Listing the stakeholders (appropriately grouped)
- Preparing a diagram showing relations between the parties involved
- Estimating the interest and influence of stakeholders
- Estimating relations.

Areas of stakeholder interest
- Stakeholder Map showing different stakeholder interests in the programme.

How to get stakeholders involved
- Depending on the circumstances, by informing, consulting and involving them in the implementation and/or decision-making
- How to ensure feedback from the stakeholders:
  - How does feedback to the programme take place
  - How are decisions made in this regard
  - How is the outcome of the feedback communicated.

Evaluating effectiveness
- How is the effectiveness of the communication measured and evaluated
- How is the perception of the stakeholders regarding the programme measured and evaluated
- How are decisions made in this regard.

Responsibilities
- The Programme Manager is responsible for preparing and implementing the Stakeholder Management Strategy
- The Programme Management Team supports the Programme Manager in preparing and carrying out the strategy
- The Senior Responsible Owner is the owner of and must approve the strategy.

Derived from
- Vision Statement
- Blueprint.

Context
- Is prepared during the DP process
- Is part of the Governing a programme
- Delivers input for the Communication Plan and the Issue Resolution Strategy

- Is input for the GP process for setting-up and managing the programme
- Defines the stakeholder management in the MP and MB processes
- Is evaluated during the tranche reviews (GP) and the CP process.

23.19 Stakeholder Map

Purpose
Providing a clear picture of the various stakeholders and their interests in the programme, with the aim of optimally managing relations with the stakeholders relevant to their interests.

The Stakeholder Map describes the various stakeholders and their interests, using a matrix showing the various stakeholders or groups of stakeholders on one side and their interests on the other.

Description
Stakeholder Map
- Matrix showing:
  - The various stakeholders
  - The various interests of the stakeholders.

It is a good idea to create groups of stakeholders, as lists of stakeholders can be very long.

Responsibilities
- The Programme Manager is responsible for preparing and updating the Stakeholder Map.

Derived from
- Vision Statement - Blueprint.

Context
- Is prepared during the DP process
- Is part of Programme Definition
- Delivers input for the Stakeholder Management Strategy and the Communication Plan
- Is input for the GP, MP and MB processes and is highlighted during these processes
- Is evaluated during the tranche reviews (GP) and the CP process.

23.20 Vision Statement

Purpose
Providing a basis to focus the attention of all involved parties on what the respective parties wish to achieve with the programme.

The Vision Statement describes the desired outcome of the programme from the client's perspective, including the forecast of new and/or improved capabilities, expressed in improved performance norms, service levels and cost reductions.

Description
End goal
- The final strategy to be achieved with the programme.

Desired results/goals
- What the programme delivers in terms of new services and/or new operational capabilities, with the performances, service levels and cost reductions to be achieved.

Responsibilities
- The Programme Manager is responsible for preparing, monitoring and updating the Vision Statement
- The Senior Responsible Owner is owner of the Vision Statement
- The Sponsoring Group must approve the Vision Statement.

Derived from
- Business strategy and policy
- Business skills
- Programme Mandate
- Programme Brief.

Context
- Is prepared during the DP process
- Is part of the Programme Definition
- Is evaluated during the MB process, the tranche reviews (GP) and the CP process.

24 Literature list

Managing Successful Programmes
This is the basic book of the MSP method and describes the structure and methods of approach to programme management.
Author: Office of Government Commerce
Publisher: The Stationery Office ISBN: 0-11-330917-1

An introduction to Programme Management
Author: Office of Government Commerce
Publisher: The Stationery Office
ISBN: 0-11-330611-3

Managing Successful Projects with PRINCE2
This is the basic book of the PRINCE2 method and describes the structure and methods of approach to project management.
Author: Office of Government Commerce
Publisher: The Stationery Office
ISBN: 0-11-330891-4

Management of Risk: Guidance for Practitioners
This is the basic book of the MoR method and describes analysing and managing risks in projects and programmes in detail.
Author: Office of Government Commerce
Publisher: The Stationery Office
ISBN: 0-11-330909-0

How to manage Business Change
This book describes the most important issues in implementing changes and how to deal with resistance during the changes.
Author: Office of Government Commerce
Publisher: The Stationery Office ISBN: 1-903091-10-1

Business Benefits through Project Management
This book describes how organizations embed the necessary skills for project management into their business processes and culture.
Author: Office of Government Commerce
Publisher: The Stationery Office
ISBN: 0-11-330891-1

25 Reference list

1. Projectmatig werken
Authors: Gert Wijnen, Willem Renes & Peter Storm
Publisher: Het Spectrum
ISBN: 9027469059

2. De weg naar projectsucces
Author: Teun van Aken
Publisher: Reed business information ISBN: 9059011538

3. Project management, an introduction based on PRINCE2
Authors: Hans Fredriksz, Bert Hedeman, Gabor Vis van Heemst
Publisher: Van Haren Publishing
ISBN: 9077212116

4. Nederlandse Competence Baseline
Author: Redactieraad PMI-NL
Publisher: Projectmanagement Instituut Nederland

5. Projecten leiden
Authors: Geert Groote, Corian Hugenholtz-Sasse, Piet Slikker and others
Publisher: Het Spectrum
ISBN: 9027468788

6. Information Economics
Author: M.M. Parker, R.J. Benson
Publisher: Prentice Hall
ISBN: 013465014X

7. Programmamanagement, sturen op samenhang
Authors: G. Wijnen, Theo van der Tak
Publisher: Het Spectrum
ISBN: 9014092938

8. Ondernemen binnen de onderneming
Authors: Mathieu Weggeman, Gert Wijnen, Rudy Kor
Publisher: Kluwer
ISBN: 9014070764

9. How to manage Business Change
Author: Office of Government Commerce
Publisher: The Stationery Office
ISBN: 190 3091101

10. Leren Veranderen
Author: Léon de Caluwé, Hans Vermaak
Publisher: Kluwer
ISBN   9014 0615 7

11. Resolving social conflicts; selected papers on group dynamics
Author: Kurt Lewin
Publisher: Harper & Row (New York)

12. Developmental sequence in small groups
Author: Bruce W. Tuckman
Publisher: Psychological Bulletin, 63, 1965

13. Levels of Existence: An Open System Theory of Values
Author: Clare W. Graves
Publisher: Journal of Humanistic Psychology, November, 1970

14. Leadership in change
Author: John P. Kotter
Publisher: Academic Service
ISBN: 90 5261 231 5

26 Contact addresses

The APM Group
F.A.O. Richard Pharro
Sword House
Totteridge Road
High Wycombe
Buckinghamshire HP13 6DG, United Kingdom
Tel: +44 (0) 1494 452450
Fax: +44 (0) 1494 459559
e-mail: info@apmgroup.co.uk

PRINCE Benelux
F.A.O. Ms. M.J. van der Deijl
PO Box 3031
1270 EA Huizen, the Netherlands
Tel: +31 (0) 35 523 1845
Fax: +31 (0) 35 523 1021
e-mail: princebenelux@cs.com

Best Practice User Group Ltd,
15 Nursery Close,
Atworth,
Melksham,
Wiltshire SN12 8HX, United Kingdom
Tel: +44 (0) 845 0548038
Fax: +44 (0) 870 131 4210
e-mail: admin@usergroup.ork.uk

MSP-User-group Nederland
F.A.O. Mr W. Wijns, Secretary p/a NedTrain Services
PO Box 2167
3500 GD Utrecht, the Netherlands
Tel: +31 (0) 30 3004915
Fax: +31 (0) 30 3004982
e-mail: info@mspug.nl

PMI Nederland PO
Box 1058
3860 BB Nijkerk, the Netherlands
Tel: +31 (0) 33 2473408
Fax: +31 (0) 33 2460470
e-mail: pminl@mos-net.nl

27 Index

This index is in alphabetical, word by word order. It does not cover the colophon, foreword, contents list or guide. Location references are to page number, e.g. Association of Project Management Group (APMG), address 241 indicates that the address for the Association of Project Management Group can be found on page 241. Where a page number is given in **bold**, this refers to the definition as given in the Definition List.

Abbreviations: Fig = figure; Tab = table

Related titles from Van Haren Publishing

For more details and sample please visit our bookshop at www.vanharen.net

Languages available: English, Dutch

PROJECT MANAGEMENT: best practice based on PRINCE2®

PRINCE2 is guidance developed by the UK Government (OGC) to support projects being developed to time and to budget. Since inception in the 1990s it has become widely adopted, including: Barclays Bank, the UN, UK Department of Work and Pensions, UK National Health Service, Australian Defence.

Project Management - an Introduction based on PRINCE2

This book takes a practical approach and is designed for those working on projects and also taking the Foundation exam. In this book, the process-based approach to project management is described and the components and techniques necessary for this are dealt with. The description of the processes, components and techniques are based on the PRINCE2 methodology. This book deals not only with the PRINCE2 methodology, but also with activities and planning resources and the project environment.